NOBODY
WANTS
TO TALK
ABOUT IT

NOBODY WANTS TO TALK ABOUT IT

RACE, IDENTITY, AND THE DIFFICULTIES IN FORGING MEANINGFUL CONVERSATIONS

MICHAEL SIDNEY FOSBERG

INCOGNITO, INC., CHICAGO

Published by Incognito, Inc., Chicago, IL
312.563.1326
www.incognitotheplay.com

Book and cover design by Tom Greensfelder.

ISBN 978-0-578-66287-9

Printed in the United States of America.

To anyone and everyone who has ever felt *different* or that they didn't belong.

We have much in common!

CONTENTS

NOBODY WANTS TO TALK ABOUT IT

Let's Start at The Beginning

We have to get our stories right from the very beginning. Part of any discussion of race has to do with how we tell the story.

CORNEL WEST

HOPE ON A TIGHTROPE

I t was early spring of 2019 and I found myself standing in a rather large, beautifully historic room at a significant federal agency in Washington, DC. I was there to perform a one-man play . . . yes, you read that correctly, I was to perform a one-man play for a group of federal employees in this extraordinarily ornate space. They had set up a makeshift stage with drapery as a backdrop and chairs fanned out in semicircles facing the stage area. I was here on the invitation of the director of diversity and inclusion, with whom I'd had a long-standing business relationship over the past several years. Like many government agencies, she'd told me, there is a great deal of pomp and circumstance surrounding visits by speakers and presenters. Mine was no exception.

Upon completion of my set-up for the show, I was whisked into another elaborately decorated and equally historic room to participate in the obligatory photo op with a senior administrator from the agency. I had been through this routine on a previous visit a few years earlier with the most senior leader of the agency and was aware of the smiling, handshaking, small-talking nature of these meetings. However, prior to this meeting, I was warned by my host that this particular administrator was not a big fan of her work. He had pushed back on the importance of diversity and saw efforts to create a workplace of inclusion as divisive at best. So when I met him, I was determined to win him over, utilizing the lessons I'd learned over years of traveling, performing, and meeting people with doubts like his. I would find out who he is, what his story is, and search for commonalities.

We jovially did the smiling and handshaking as we discussed my visit and unusual approach, a one-man show as a speech on diversity. He spoke about his life in the private sector and how he'd spent time out on the West Coast—a connection I made almost immediately—and talked with great enthusiasm about a commitment to making a difference in government. I expressed my admiration toward his sentiments about using his position to make a difference and pointed out our common goal, mine through the use of my play, that is, my life story. He became rather animated and exuberant during our conversation, and I could feel a definite connection being forged.

When it came time for my presentation, my host asked the administrator if he still wanted to make some comments to the employees who had gathered to see my show before I started, as had been the original plan. He turned to me and asked how long my piece was, and I informed him it was forty-five minutes, with an additional thirty minutes of post-show Q&A. He smiled, thought for a moment, then said he might stay and watch a bit. He would sit in the back, so he could come and go without being a distraction, and suggested that when the time was appropriate, he'd return to give some closing remarks instead. I was taken aback (as was my host)—it had been my experience, having done presentations in numerous federal agencies, that head administrators rarely have time to stay and watch these types of programs . . . especially a one-man play! These are busy people with a lot on their plate.

So with that, we headed back into the beautifully ornate historic room now masquerading as a converted theater space. My host gave me a brief introduction and I commenced to perform my auto-biographical one-man play in front of an audience of some seventy -five rapt federal employees. The nature of the presentation (more on that in a minute) allows me to speak directly to audience members throughout the play, so I literally watch them as they watch me. I witness audience members laughing, contemplating, looking puzzled, and sometimes struggling with different aspects of the story. The play contains sharply comedic moments, heart-wrenching emotional issues, and challenging identity questions, which I get to watch audience members wrestle with in real time.

By the time I finished the show that morning, I was dumb-struck as the group rose in applause, including the administrator, who had not left the room once I began. He sat riveted the entire time and rose in unison with the audience when I delivered my final lines. The audience's enthusiasm carried over into the dialogue which always follows my presentations and led to the administrator rising in his chair and approaching the stage to offer his closing remarks. With a smile plastered broadly across his face, he thanked me profusely, imploring the audience to reciprocate. He continued by saying what a remarkable thing they'd all just experienced, one not soon to be forgotten, and how it might not be hyperbole to call this particular story a life-changing event for all. I could tell he was deeply moved and shaken by the story and the resulting dialogue as he struggled to put into words the strong emotions he felt.

Then, out of the blue, he held up his phone to me and said: "There's another remarkable similarity we share. I too had hair like yours when I was young. I guess you would call it . . ." and he faded off, unsure if it was proper for him to utter the term most often used to describe his wild and curly Jewish hair.

"You had a Jewfro!" I shouted gleefully, gazing at the faded photo displayed on his phone's screen. And we both roared with laughter as I then reached out and offered a soul handshake which he enthusiastically returned. The audience roared back with laughter and the moment was sealed. We had connected on a deep level, and it was my personal story that took him along on his own ride with identity.

I was told later by my host that at a senior-level staff meeting the following day this administrator stood up in front of the entire roomful of leaders and praised the program he had seen the previous day. The one in which he rediscovered his Jewfro from the past and the commonalities he shared with a guy (me) who looked just like him but didn't actually have a Jewfro but something else entirely.

So what is this Jewfro, not Jewfro I speak of, and how was it I found myself in front of an audience of federal employees performing an autobiographical one-man play? Well, as this administrator pointed out in his closing remarks to my audience, I had experienced a life-changing event that led me there.

* * * *

In 1993 I made a phone call that inadvertently changed the course of my life. This remarkable phone call began a search to track down the biological father I'd never known and wound up changing not only my identity but also the direction my life and career would take.

Having grown up in a working-class White family in the northern suburbs of Chicago, I was more or less unprepared for what was about to unfold. I was raised by my biological Armenian mother and adopted by my Swedish stepfather, and my parents had two more children. I was blessed with a fairly normal White household. My parents worked diligently, each holding down full-time jobs while raising three children on their path to the middle class. Although my appearance was distinctively different from my stepfather and his offspring (my siblings)—my kinky, wild hair and olive complexion contrasted sharply to their straight locks and fair skin—we all shared a trademark grin along with an optimistic exuberance. There were aunts and uncles, numerous cousins, and boisterous family gatherings. Toss in a hearty helping of Armenian heritage from my mother's side and the extended family seemed to grow with each annual church picnic. It was a childhood filled with delicious Armenian dishes, neighborhoods filled with kids, and occasional trips north to Wisconsin's well-traversed family tourist destinations for the affordable working-class vacation.

Those childhood memories safe, I was well into my adult years when I found my family stability shaken. In my early thirties my parents unexpectedly announced that they had filed for a divorce, this on the heels of constructing a sizable new home in a tonier neighborhood. My family dynamic now shaken, I suddenly realized I knew nothing about my biological father whom my mother had left when I was barely two. A healthy dose of fear had kept me from asking the important questions when I was growing up, questions for which I now found myself seeking answers. The fear of water that stunted my swimming abilities, along with being scared of fielding a sharply hit ground ball which contributed to my embarrassing failure in Little League, created anxiety over rocking the boat in my family by asking questions about a father no one had acknowledged, let alone spoken about. At the time I had a British girlfriend who, in a nod to her own personal history growing up without a father, encouraged me to confront my mother. In an unsteady phone conversation with my mother, she divulged a name and the city in which my biodad had lived some thirty years prior. Armed with a newfound sense of purpose, this being the days before we used the internet for everything, I visited the reference section of my local library where I discovered a collection of telephone directories from various cities across the country.

I selected the Detroit directory, looked up his name, then copied down the five listings I discovered. I dashed from the library, racing the six blocks home in a daze, anxious about taking the next step on my quest. When I arrived home, I paced the three steps across and two steps back my one-room rent-controlled apartment would allow, attempting to calm my nerves. What if I found him? What would I say? What if he didn't want to speak with me? What if none of the names on the list were my father? Finally, I placed the names and numbers on the table in front of me, picked up the phone, and dialed the first listing. A man answered.

"Hello?"

I was taken aback upon hearing a deeply familiar resonant voice.

"Hi, I'm looking for a John Sidney Woods."

There was a long pause.

"You're speaking with him," he responded with his low smooth drawl.

It couldn't be that easy, I told myself. *Could this be the guy? What should I ask next?*

"D . . . did . . . did you live in the Boston area in 1957?" I sputtered. My mother and I had lived there with my dad right after I was born. He paused again, for what seemed like an hour.

"Yes, I did."

Desperate to prove this was my father beyond a doubt, I'd devised one more question sure to nail down his identity.

"W . . . w . . . were you married to a woman by the name of Adrienne Pilibosian?" Invoking my mother's distinctive Armenian maiden name would certainly cast any remaining doubts aside.

Again he paused, for what now seemed like an eternity.

"Yes . . . I was," came his steady affirmation.

I had found my biological father with the first phone call thirty years later! I blurted out, "My name is Michael Fosberg, and I'm your son!"

So here we were, thirty years gone by, father and son. What do we say? How do we proceed? He told me he was married to a woman named Sue, I told him I was living in LA, near the beach in Santa Monica. He asked me about my apartment—which, if it were possible, suddenly shrank in size. Then he said, "You know, son"—a word that should have been expected but still stopped me in my tracks—"there's a couple of things you should know I'm sure your mother never told you."

Aside from not telling me about him, I thought, what on earth could he be talking about?

"Like what?" I asked softly with slight trepidation.

He began with, "First of all I want you to know that no matter what you were told, or thought had happened, I have always loved you and thought about you a lot." My father, telling me for the first time in memory that he loved me—I felt such incredible joy and sorrow in that moment. "There's one other thing I'm sure your mother's never told you." As I waited, unable to breathe (was I holding my breath?), he said, "I'm African American."

I don't really remember what I thought I was expecting to hear. It most certainly was not that. There was a full-length mirror affixed to the door of the only closet in my tiny one-room apartment.

I remember glancing at myself in the mirror while trying to steady the phone to my ear. Had I changed? I cannot even begin to describe the jumble of thoughts that now raced through my mind as I stood there in that cramped room attempting to process what I had just heard, what I had just discovered. It was probably only a few seconds—amazing the speed at which our minds race—but it may have seemed like forever to him, as he asked, "Are you okay?"

"Yeah . . . I'm good, I'm great," I stammered. "She never bothered to mention that!"

He continued, "Your great-great-grandfather was a member of the Fifty-Fourth Regiment in the colored infantry unit during the Civil War. Your great-grandfather, Charles "Lefty" Robinson, was an all-star pitcher in the Negro Leagues. The science and engineering building at Norfolk State University is named after your grandfather. Both your grandparents are still alive and living in Virginia Beach, Virginia. Your grandmother has four siblings, all still alive and well."

How could I have not known?

I felt dizzy as we talked about meeting, exchanged contact information, and swore we'd stay in touch. Hanging up the phone I thought, *Why hadn't my mother told me?*

My mind was on overload trying to sort through all the implications. I started in on the what if's and if only's: If only I had known before I filled out applications for college! What if my British girlfriend wouldn't accept my new-found blackness? How do I go about telling my family? What about my friends? How would they see me now? Most importantly, how do I see myself? Have I changed? Am I different? What am I?

I'm sure there are many who might question why this revelation would change the course of my life and work. It's a legitimate question to be sure. I was raised White, appeared (to most people)

White, and benefited from the advantages of that privilege. Why should it make any difference to me what my biodad was? How does that actually change my life? I suppose one could argue that simply the discovery of a long-lost parent might be ground-shaking in itself, but in what way does race play a factor?

I didn't set out to do what came next—it took almost ten years actually—but it was a logical path, taking into account the background I had in writing and acting. Early in 2001 I began working on a one-man play recounting the story of the search for my biological father, the discovery of my African American roots, and how I processed the sudden change in my life's path. The play came about through the stories I had been jotting down for a memoir I was attempting to write. I titled the play *Incognito*, which seemed apt given my own deception of identity. Initially I performed the play in a few theaters around the Midwest, and much to my surprise something strange and wonderful began to unfold.

During a run of the show at a large regional theater, I'd been contracted to do a couple of morning performances for groups of high school students bussed in to see the play. Following each of these, it is customary for the performers to meet with the students to answer questions and discuss the artistic process involved in creating the work. What happened during these sessions made me realize that the story was exposing something deeper. The student audiences were relating to the story on a universal level, that is, they began to contemplate and talk about how they perceived themselves and others. The play created an opening for dialogue on race, identity, stereotypes, and family history. I was bombarded with questions about racial categories, stereotypes, and cultural differences. I was sought out especially by those in the audience who were biracial, a growing number, seeking advice and counsel on how to navigate the tricky boundaries of race and identity.

Soon after this experience I began to be invited to perform at various high schools across the country, following each presentation with a similar facilitated dialogue about these delicate and often ignored issues. Each year the list of schools grew longer, and colleges started calling once I became acquainted with an agency that booked presentations, or "social issues lectures," as they are called in that market. After a presentation at a business college during their annual Black History Month celebration (a month for which my show is in constant demand), I found myself speaking with representatives from area corporations inquiring about my availability to present and engage their employees in the meaningful post-show dialogue.

Across the various groups there was often a set of similar questions that seemed to rise to the top: How do we come to understand who we are? How do we look at other people? Why do other people see us differently than we see ourselves? However, there were also troubling things that came up. Students at literally every college campus I visited shared stories of racist, homophobic, and gender discriminatory events that had taken place. Minorities expressed feeling marginalized by lack of an inclusive environment and a general discomfort in carrying on a discussion about race and identity in mixed company.

It was during this time that I ran across an article describing a theory that resonated profoundly with the work I was doing. Intergroup contact theory, devised by Gordon W. Allport, a Harvard psychologist, during the '50s, proved that by sharing our personal stories across majority and minority populations we could break down the prejudices that exist between us by discovering we had more in common than we were different.[1] His theory speaks

[1] Gordon W. Allport, *The Nature of Prejudice* (New York: Perseus Books, 1979; originally published in 1954).

to the power of storytelling in which universal human experience is shared by all.

As I embarked on adding corporations to my growing list of clients, I also began to read and study everything I could get my hands on that dealt with issues of race and identity. I wanted to be able not only to facilitate thorough and meaningful post-show dialogues but also to connect the dots to my personal story and those of others. I found people were not only fascinated by the details of my personal journey but equally engrossed in the discourse about how we see ourselves. Is it color of skin that defines us? Our culture, our heritage, religion, the foods we eat, the music we listen to, the clothes we wear, the accent we speak with? And does this path of identity shift as we grow older?

Each year, as the list of venues and clients grew, I found myself dashing from state to state provoking dialogues and helping people sort through identity issues. Sharing my story—in dramatic form—was not only cathartic, but bridge building. As I toured, making friends and changing lives, I frantically worked on transforming my story into book form, and in 2011 *Incognito: An American Odyssey of Race and Self-Discovery* was published. The book explores the larger story of my discovery, along with the perplexing questions about race, identity, adoption, father-son relationships, and family history and secrets.

In fifteen years of touring I have spoken to thousands of people, conducted workshops and training sessions for students and corporations, given keynote addresses at conferences, and done interviews with the media. I have written about and advocated for dialogue about these issues as a way to create a bridge to understanding one another. But the difficult questions remain unanswered and are still seldom discussed.

What is race? What is our experience with race? Why does

race matter? Should it matter? Why is it important to talk about race? Can dialogue about race be beneficial? Does race play an important role in how we judge people or how we communicate with people? How do we define racism? Why is there discrimination? What constructive tools can be used to have a (civil) dialogue about race? How do you self-identify? How do we arrive at our identities?

Today there are people talking about race and identity all across the country, from the media to academics, students, and even the occasional politician. I would not have such an active tour schedule if this weren't the case (on average I do sixty presentations each year). However, the way in which race and identity is discussed—or talked around—shows a true lack of understanding (and fear) of each other's identity, culture, or heritage. Additionally the type of language used in speaking to one another is steeped in hundreds of years of unconscious shame (slavery), awkward attempts (lack of cultural understanding), and disrespectful, often coded, rhetoric (use of the N-word, discussing welfare moochers, or labeling President Obama "the most divisive socialist Muslim"), so it's no wonder we struggle when asked to have civil dialogue in mixed company.

There are, of course, people who steadfastly believe that dialogue about race and identity is a ridiculous idea, isn't needed, and can't possibly help solve what they do not see as a problem. Many think we've had far too much talk about race and that further discourse is truly a waste of time. Polls show that a majority of White people think issues centered around race are far better in our country today, while a majority of people of color still think there is vastly more work to be done. That alone says a good deal about how Blacks and Whites have drastically different views of the issue. Add to this the nature of what passes today for dialogue—Facebook posts, Twitter, and comment sections following articles on news websites—and it is obvious we woefully lack the will to sit down face to face and get comfortable with the uncomfortable.

The volatility has increased over the past few years as the explosion of videos of Black men, women, and children unjustifiably shot by police are exposed, with the emergence of the Black Lives Matter movement, and as racial and identity politics on college campuses has risen to fever pitch. These harsh inequalities have fermented in a climate of fear, resentment, and nationalism stoked by a hostile, brutish, and divisive president and an administration perhaps unlike any our nation has ever seen.

This hyper-partisan climate is the backdrop for deeply troubling statistics between Blacks and Whites:

- A much higher unemployment rate for people of color
- Hugely disparate health care access and outcomes
- Huge disparities in household wealth
- Overrepresentation of people of color in the prison population relative to percentage of population
- Unavailability of home mortgages and financing
- Voting rights under attack

I could go on, but statistics can be cold, cruel, and not easily personalized for those they do not affect.

Squeezed between the bad news and unequal realities, my show, my story, has provided a space to find common ground with one another. This, the opening salvo if you will, can help us return to the idea of talking *to* one another rather than *at* one another. Over the course of nearly a thousand performances of my play I've learned a great deal from acting (*living* is probably a more appropriate term) as a facilitator of conscious authentic dialogue. This work has given me a front-row seat—sometimes a not too comfortable one—in the effort to get folks talking. I've been in a position to learn a great many things and had the privilege to share those lessons in the hope of helping others.

Writing a book invites criticism, writing one about race guarantees it. So, why write a book about race if there are so many people who think they've already talked about the topic enough, aren't interested in anything outside their own world, and probably wouldn't ever bother to pick it up and read it? Because if we give up, give in, don't bother, stop trying, or lose hope, then we'll always be at each other's throats. However, if one person who reads this book (a chapter, a page, a paragraph . . . hell, one sentence!) is moved by it enough to think about how they see themselves and others, then perhaps they can share their experience, their story, and affect another. I have always felt deeply connected to people from all walks of life, in many parts of the globe. I may not always agree with a person's politics, way of life, or vision of the world, but I choose to see the vast similarities between us as outweighing the small number of differences. These commonalities connect us as human beings on a level so deep that many people are unaware of the significance this holds. If we choose to become aware, conscious of these profound connections, they can significantly change the way we congregate, communicate, and collaborate on a global scale.

Finally, what makes me an expert to hold forth opinion and proffer dialogue on these sensitive topics? What makes anyone an expert? I don't profess to know all there is to know, hold all the answers to the questions I'm asking, or portray myself as some kind of biracial spokesperson. I am a guy who grew up thinking he was White and who discovered later in life that I am much more than I seem. Over and over I have witnessed my story resonating with many people in a way that is universal and allows them to open up to discuss matters of identity in a safe and personal way. I have a great passion for what I do and feel blessed to be able to conduct such probing conversations through the use of theater arts. As a biracial individual I—along with many others—have a unique opportunity to be a bridge. I can help folks forge a bridge, a connection across race, ethnicity, sexual orientation, and other perceived differences. During all this talk of building walls, we—biracial people—can build bridges.

The topic of race and identity is not mathematics or science. There isn't a formula that adds up each time to the same conclusion. It's not $a + b = c$, or what have you. Race and identity are emotional issues, and although there are many who have vast resources of education and knowledge, these issues don't have an exact method. Like most things emotional, there are individual differences dictated by one's experience in life. Each of us approaches the issues from our own unique perspective. Therefore I believe there are no experts in this field, simply people who continue to do the deep work day in and day out. Some may have a little more knowledge and a little less experience. Some may have a little less knowledge and a little more experience. All are committed to the work of trying to build bridges, creating environments that are more diverse and inclusive.

The conversation about race and identity in mixed company is fraught with problems and a general sense of uncomfortableness. White people approach the conversation from a place of caution. Some more than others are hesitant to say anything that might make them sound racist, at worst, or at least insensitive. They have also rarely had conversations about race growing up since race is not something most White people have to deal with on a daily basis. Many people of color are ready to pounce on anyone or anything that sounds remotely racist. They feel anger and resentment, having tried for years to forge this conversation only to be rebuffed ("now's not the time"), belittled ("we talk about it too much"), and disrespected ("slavery happened a long time ago, get over it!"). As a result we are polarized and rarely talk about the issues in mixed company. And although race is the major strain of this book, identity in general is something many people grapple with in negative ways. Gender, sexual orientation, disability, age, religion, and nationality can all be factors in the way people accept or reject us. Talking about these traits can incite avoidance, silence, and even inappropriate or offensive responses.

After literally hundreds of presentations and in-depth dialogues, including many awkward conversations, I assembled a set of tools or takeaways, if you will, which I believe will be useful in navigating these uncomfortable conversations:

1. Tell your story. Open up and listen. By sharing our personal stories we discover commonalities.

2. Don't judge the differences. Flip the script; instead of allowing the differences to create a wall between us, start by finding a mutual interest, then embrace the differences. (After all, if we were all the same, we'd be bored!) It's the differences that make us stand out as people, and it's the differences that make us unique in the marketplace.

3. Recognize that there isn't any one way to have a conversation about identity and race. We all have different experiences and therefore bring different points of view to the table—this is actually the strength of our collective spirit, our diversity.

4. We can disagree, so long as we're not disagreeable. Take responsibility for the language we use—freedom of speech carries responsibilities.
5. Get comfortable being uncomfortable.
6. Understand that there are realities outside your own experience. Just because we may not have experienced racism, sexism, homophobia, age discrimination, disability indifference, or other forms of discriminatory treatment doesn't mean those are not realities for other people. Listen with empathy.
7. Practice forgiveness. It has been described as the hardest work you will ever do but the most rewarding.

Thus, my goal with this book is to share stories from across a wide range of venues and clients, while offering the tools I learned from these experiences, which we can all use in our efforts to become more united, find common ground, and talk across barriers that currently separate us. Each chapter is titled after a tool and includes the stories with which I discovered that particular take-away. These are by no means an exhaustive list of things we can do or use to have a more productive and civil conversation about race and identity. These are merely starting points. There are many dedicated people out there trying to forge difficult conversations using a myriad of methods and tools. My hope is that these tools, this book, will add to the arsenal of valuable methods in use today.

✵ ✵ ✵ ✵

A note on the use of the words *White* and *Black*: I have chosen to capitalize these words much like one would in utilizing the words

Asian, Hispanic, or any other ethnicity or nationality. And although my message is one that tries not to promote a one-size-fits-all racial, ethnic, or national category, I use the terms *White* and *Black* freely, knowing full well there is a vast variety of ways that folks within these categories would describe themselves.

And a note on names and institutions: For the sake of privacy and anonymity, I have shielded most names of people and institutions except where absolutely necessary for context of the story.

The people who see me as white always will, and will think it's madness that anyone else could come to any other conclusion, holding to this falsehood regardless of learning my true identity. The people who see me as black cannot imagine how a sane, intelligent person could be so blind not to understand this, despite my pale-skinned presence. The only influence I have over this perception, if any, is in the initial encounter. Here is my chance to be categorized as black, with an asterisk. The asterisk is my whole body.

MAT JOHNSON
LOVING DAY

ONE

Tell Your Story

*As time passed, I found that these stories, taken together,
had helped me bind my world together, that they gave me a sense
of place and purpose I'd been looking for. Marty was right:
There was always a community there if you dug deep enough.*

BARACK OBAMA

*DREAMS FROM MY FATHER:
A STORY OF RACE AND INHERITANCE*

While visiting an affluent, primarily White public school in the northern suburbs of Chicago, an odd thing happened over the course of the day. I was scheduled to perform three shows for the students—two during the morning and one in the afternoon. Three shows in one day was brutally exhausting since the play requires a great deal of energy and focus over the course of fifty minutes. I was excited, however, and the younger me (this was early on in my touring days) was up for the challenge. I arrived at the school early to set up and did some vocal and physical warm-ups, and I was slightly nervous but ready when the first group of students began filing into the room.

During that first show I noticed a tall Black gentleman enter at the back of the room, where he stood leaning against the wall. As the play unfolded, the students seemed to be engaged and focused. They laughed freely at the funnier parts and got intensely quiet during the moments of self-reflection. I thought I'd noticed the tall gentleman smiling during the moments with my Black family. During the post-show conversations with the students, as I encouraged them to confront their own stereotypes and perceptions, I could see the tall Black gentleman nodding his head. The talkback grew especially lively as the students delved into the issue of identity designations—how we use specific terms to describe ambiguous-looking people. They were puzzled about the concept of race and why we utilize labels with check boxes on forms. A White student asked me what it now felt like to be African American, carefully selecting a term that seemed to him to be socially more acceptable than, say, Black. I asked him what it felt like to be White, and he stumbled as he tried to put it into words. I tried to help him understand also that the way he sees himself is different from the way other White students in his class see themselves, and thus, although we may share certain traits within our racial groups, there is no one way or experience for Blacks or Whites.

At this point, I needed to wrap up the dialogue as I had only about fifteen minutes between shows to reset the stage, get a drink of water, and take a short breather. As the students filed out, buzz-ing with questions between themselves, I began the task of resetting the stage to prepare for round two. The tall gentleman approached me as the last students filed out of the auditorium, and as he stood in front of me at the edge of the stage I realized he was a custodian, dressed in a standard industrial outfit, clean gray shirt, black slacks, black shoes. I said hello and he nodded back, then said, "That's some story you got there."

"Yes . . . I know . . . it's been quite a journey," I replied.

"Do you perform it often?" he inquired.

"Well, yes, as a matter of fact, I travel around the country to various high schools and colleges presenting the show and attempt-ing to engage students in meaningful dialogue."

"Ever'body needs to hear your story."

"Why, thank you, yes, I am trying to get to as many schools as will have me."

"No, I mean ever'body here needs to hear your message. It's important and could go a long way in helping people understand one another. We're not so different."

His simple statement couldn't have been truer, but that's not what we'd been teaching in our schools and elsewhere, nor have I seen this change in the many years since that presentation. We smiled and shook hands as I thanked him for stopping to talk. As he left, I quickly finished my setup and within moments was greeting a new audience. About fifteen minutes into the second performance, I noticed the door opening at the back of the auditorium and in walked two Black women who stood against the rear wall, much like the gentleman had earlier. Both women were clearly dressed in uniforms one might find cafeteria workers wearing. As they watched and enjoyed the show and then the dialogue, I surmised it was the gentleman who visited me earlier who had told them about the show. This repeated itself during my third and final performance that afternoon when four Black adults found their way to my play. Again, dressed in uniforms, I sensed they were there not only to hear my story but to see and hear how the students responded to it.

These extra audience members of color stood out from the exclusively White teaching staff and predominantly White student body. All were there to hear a personal story, one that seemed to resonate in different ways to different people. Yet all were relating to the universal idea of a shared human experience.

* * * *

One night after a show during the run of my play at the Kansas City Repertory Theatre (formerly the Missouri Repertory Theatre), the stage manager came into my dressing room to inform me that I had a couple of guests waiting for me outside the theater's greenroom (the actors' backstage lounge—or, in this case, the lone actor's solitary retreat!). I didn't know anyone in KC so I was extra curious as to who might have made the trek here in order to catch the show. As I exited the greenroom into the hallway connecting the backstage area to the lobby, I was met by a young couple I did not recognize. I guessed they may have been in their late twenties, dressed properly for a night out at the theater. The woman approached me first as I walked toward them. She was White with long blond hair and a warm but somewhat melancholy smile. She reached out her hand, and I offered an appreciative hello.

"Mr. Fosberg, thank you so much for meeting us. We loved your show, your play, I mean," she stumbled. and the man leaned toward her. I took her extended hand and thanked them, glancing over at the man, whose eyes were red and glazed over. "This is my husband," she added. "He wanted to meet you . . . we did. Your story . . . it . . . well, it moved us quite deeply." She let go of my hand as I turned to look at her husband, who was now fighting back his tears with all he had in him. He wore a nicely tailored suit under his overcoat, which he tugged at with his hands, clearly uncomfortable. I immediately noticed his close-cropped hair and what I can only describe as tanned skin tone. I waited patiently for him to speak but could see that was going to be difficult, if not impossible. He could barely make eye contact with me as he stumbled forward, desperately attempting to hold back his tears.

"I . . . you . . . I wanted to . . ." he started, but found each attempt blocked by a strong deeply emotional source.

"He found your story truly inspiring," his wife squeezed in, and he nodded his head slowly to acknowledge the truth of her statement.

I gazed at him quietly, gently offering a space to experience the full weight of his feelings, and I saw in him what was part of me. He was clearly, to me anyway, a biracial person who had just experienced his story told for the first time. As he fumbled again to make sense, searching for language he did not have at his disposal, I reached out, grabbed his hand, and hugged him with my other arm. Not quite the traditional Black man's hug, as I did not pat him with my hugging arm but rather grasped and held him firmly. His body contracted slightly, and I could feel him gasp for air, weeping silently for a moment in my embrace.

When I released my grip, he wiped his eyes and face, then sniffled as he said, or rather choked out, "Thank you. It means a lot to me." I glanced over at his wife, now smiling radiantly with tears looping down her bright pink cheeks, and told them how honored I was to have them seek me out and share their joy and pain. It was a moment I will never forget . . . that moment when you realize how powerful your personal story is on a universal level.

✳ ✳ ✳ ✳

Much earlier, during the first run of my play at a theater in Chicago, I was approached by a middle-aged White woman asking if we could talk. She had long dark hair that sort of hid her face but couldn't conceal the urgency I saw in her eyes.

"Sure," I told her.

She wondered if there was a place we could speak which might give us more privacy. I looked around the ninety-nine-seat theater, now empty, and suggested we might sit in the back. We made our way into a dark corner at the back of the house, sat across the aisle from one another, and properly introduced ourselves. She spoke softly but had trouble making direct eye contact, hiding behind the veil of her long hair, looking off to one side then back, perhaps hoping I wouldn't notice.

"I so thoroughly enjoyed your show." She smiled gently. "I found I could relate to quite a bit of what your mother went through. She had to make some very difficult decisions at such an early age. It must have been hard for her." Again she had difficulty meeting my eyes. She was obviously a bit uncomfortable.

"Yes," I replied, "she didn't have a lot of help back then. I know she wishes she could have done things differently, but I try to remind her that things worked out the way they did, and it turned out pretty well."

For a moment things seemed lopsided, as if she were carrying a weight she was unable to shed. I, on the other hand, had left my weight on stage by sharing my story in its theatrical form and opening the door for her to approach me. I could tell she was trying to figure out where to go next with the conversation, so I waited politely, cautiously.

"I wonder if I might ask your advice?" she asked kindly.

"Absolutely," I said, a bit too confident, unaware of what door I may have opened.

Looking away again, she began. "I've been married to a wonderful man for ten years, and we have two adorable children, three and five. A couple of months ago my husband came out to me and revealed he was gay. I was quite taken aback and I've been trying to sort through my thoughts and feelings ever since. We still care for each other deeply and we feel it's best to give each other an opportunity to be happy. We've committed to splitting up in order for both of us to move on. Our main concern, of course, is how all this will affect our children. They will most likely live with me, but he'll need to have a role in their lives as well. He loves them both deeply, but he plans to move out of state, so his involvement with the kids will be limited. What I am wondering is . . . should I tell my kids their dad is gay? You said your mother struggled and ultimately decided not to tell you about your father being African American." She brought her eyes to meet mine as she posed this final question. "I know you say you've forgiven her, but . . . how do I . . . what should I . . . will my kids grow up resenting me should I withhold the truth?"

And just like that I was thrust into the role of therapist. My show, my life story rather, opened the door for a complete stranger to approach me and ask for advice about a deeply personal situation. Up until that point I had been truly unaware of the power of my story to connect with people so deeply. Unaware and unprepared.

I wanted to offer this woman some sound, quality advice; however, I recognized clearly that this was an area that needed expert opinion, expertise I was definitively lacking. "Listen," I told her, "I am not a therapist, or an expert in psychology. I'm just a guy with a story. I am so honored you would share this deeply personal side of your life with me, and I completely understand the correlation to my own, or should I say, my mother's own dilemma. However, I suggest you seek a professional to speak with, to offer you counsel. If I can say anything about what I've learned over the years spent on my own reconciliation, it's that there is no right or wrong decision. Everyone's situation is different and carries a differing set of parameters. Although I probably lean more toward the old adage, 'honesty is the best policy,' sometimes there are extenuating circumstances which make it difficult or hurtful to share the entire story. My mother clearly did not know what to do or say. What would her three-year-old child comprehend? And at what age would it have made sense? At four? Five? Seven? Ten? Obviously once she hesitated and life—a new husband, two more kids, et cetera—moved along, it became more and more difficult for her to open up. But times and circumstances were different. Your decision requires help I'm afraid I am unqualified to offer." I urged her to seek a professional who could help her sort through her various options, thanked her again for coming, and wished her well, hoping she was not put off by my reticence to advise. She seemed almost relieved as she thanked me and offered more praise for both my courage and talents. I thanked her again as I led her out into the lobby, waving as she exited the theater, presumably on her way home, head full of thoughts and feelings.

That conversation took place in 2001, and although nineteen years is not really that much time to have passed, it is significant. Because of huge shifts in the acceptance of gay marriage, this conversation may not be necessary today. Someone in this same situation may not feel the same reluctance to share this information with their children, especially in a large urban area. Although prejudice toward gay members of society and the taboos that surround what some see as a lifestyle choice still exist quite prominently in our country, there has been a noticeable shift toward increased acceptance.

This was, however, the first time I truly recognized how powerful my story was and how it had the capacity to open people up to deep, meaningful conversations. It was her story that made me realize I should probably prepare myself for others like her who would seek out my advice and counsel.

* * * *

During 2011–2012, I was working with a New York–based press agent who asked me to do a radio interview with a woman by the name of Bev Smith. I wasn't familiar with Ms. Smith's impressive resume, but I discovered she was (and still claims to be) the only nationally syndicated African American woman on radio . . . dubbed the Queen of Late Night Talk. They had booked me for what I thought was an unheard-of thirty-minute slot, and owing to my busy tour schedule, I was to call in from my hotel room some-where on the road.

It is probably worth mentioning here that most interviews, be it radio or television, are usually ridiculously short . . . sound-bite short! If they give you five minutes to talk about your story or (God forbid!) race, you are incredibly lucky. Much like people in general, the media don't really want to talk about race, and when they do, they almost always assign a journalist of color to cover the story.

Anyway, I was warned by my press agent that I needed to sus-tain a high level of energy for my late-night interview with Bev Smith. The experience of calling in to a radio show, being put on hold for long periods of time between commercial breaks, not knowing when they'll come back to you while the phone line is dead silent, and being as lively and engaging as you possibly can at 10 p.m. in a hotel room somewhere in the middle of nowhere can be a daunting proposition. Bev Smith, however, keeps things inter-esting while on air, which makes the lively portion of the equation easy. Not having any visual clues can sometimes be confusing as well, but Bev speaks with a very authoritarian voice in a declam-atory way, which suggests a well-seasoned veteran well aware of the power of her voice over the airwaves. She's a reverend of the airwaves, in full throttle and fully in control.

So the conversation was lively, and I found her questions both probing and amusing. At a certain point she became fixated on the idea that because I'd grown up White but was now a "Black pio-neer," as she put it, I had dirt on how White people thought and spoke about Black people. She seemed to be suggesting that I had probably been present at gatherings where Whites spoke deroga-torily about Blacks. She said, "You've seen it, you've heard it, what can you tell us about how Whites talk about Blacks?"

I found this idea both humorous and disturbing. Sure, I'd heard a few racist things said from time to time in the company of White people who did not know (incognito) my true identity. However, it wasn't as if all White people said racist things about Black people all the time. It was a crazy idea. I felt like I was visiting an alternate universe from Sean Hannity or Bill O'Reilly, with their constant drone about reverse racism. With little to offer her in terms of "White talk about Blacks," she finally let the inquiry go and offered her listeners a commercial break. But before placing me on hold once again, she asked if I could talk with her for another hour!

I wasn't sure if she was enjoying the conversation, had a lot more to cover, or had lost her next guest and needed to fill the time. I figured things had gone fairly well to that point and the additional airtime could only help in getting my message out about my work, the show, and my recently published book, of which I was hoping to sell copies.

Over the course of the next hour we spoke about a great many things in relationship to my story and, of course, race relations. She continued to try to bring up the notion that most White people are saying negative things about Blacks and that I must have witnessed something. At one point, I was hammering the idea about how important it is for us to share our personal stories in order to discover our commonalities, and she mentioned something about one of her best friends being White. I was surprised by this revelation and impulsively asked how they met. She told the listeners that they'd met at some kind of social function and got to talking about their respective mothers, who both suffered from Alzheimer's. They had shared their personal struggles and grief surrounding their mothers and discovered a deeply common bond which has lasted to this day.

I couldn't help but smile as she shared this story, thinking about how she'd just tried to get me to expose the underbelly of White people's racism, then quickly shifted to a story about finding a common bond with someone who is White. One of her best friends is White and they share a deeply personal journey: doesn't that say all you need to know about making connections with people?

✲ ✲ ✲ ✲

In February 2012 I was asked to present my play as part of the Black History Month celebration at a business college outside of Philadelphia. This was a small school that wielded sizable influence with the area's numerous corporate establishments. The show was to take place in a large lecture hall on a campus located in a non-descript office park. They were excited about the evening and had a full house of RSVPs plus a long waiting list of those wishing to attend.

As I sat backstage going through my preshow ritual of vocal and physical warm-ups alone with the usual preshow anxiety, a gentleman suddenly burst backstage. A middle-aged White man, tall, well-dressed, with dark hair and frantic energy but a joyful look on his face. He quickly apologized for barging in on me then immediately started in on how he'd been dying to meet me when he'd heard my story on a local radio interview I'd given the previous day. He too had a similar story in that he recently discovered his father was Black, having not known him the entirety of his White life. He was so elated to meet me, someone who'd lived an eerily similar racial fate!

He told me about growing up White in the suburbs of Philly with his White biological mom and a stepfather and discovering just two weeks ago that his biological dad was Black. He'd spoken to his father but had yet to meet him, excited but nervous about the prospect. It was an amazing moment, but happening so fast and just moments before I was to step on stage that I had little time to really process the weight of his discovery, our connection, and the serendipity of life's path.

* * * *

So . . . the first lesson I learned on this long and winding journey is to tell your story. Open up and listen. By sharing our personal stories we discover commonalities. Utilizing the principle of inter-group contact theory, by sharing our stories, we can discover we have more in common than not, and we can thus break down some of the preconceived prejudices (unconscious biases) we all have.

I'm a firm believer that you must start any conversation about identity by sharing a bit about your own identity. Let's start with who we are and what kind of experience we have with being who we are, and, if we are aware enough, how that experience shapes the way we perceive others. If we are going to engage in a conversation about race and identity, we need to put our own experience on the table first thing so that we know who's in the room and to help others understand our experience.

The concept of identity is complex, shaped by individual char-acteristics, family dynamics, historical factors, and social and politi-cal contexts. Who am I? The answer unfortunately depends in large part on who the world around me says I am. Who do my parents say I am? Who do my peers say I am? My colleagues? What message is reflected back to me in the faces and voices of my teachers, my neighbors, store clerks, the people I work with? What do I learn from the media about myself? How am I represented in the cul-tural images around me? However, even though these are powerful influences on how I see myself, ultimately it is I who not only gets to choose but to own who I am. This is a very important aspect of our attempt to share our identity with others but often the most ignored. Do I identify with a group—a school, a sports team, a company, a religion, ethnicity, a race, gender, an age, disability, and so on? To what degree do these affect the way I see myself? We all arrive at our identities in different ways. Also, it is very important to recognize that identity is fluid; it is constantly changing. There are obviously some things about us that do not change: our skin color, our nationality, perhaps our gender; however, the ways in which we identify those things may shift over our lives. (I have seen myself as White, then Armenian, then Black, and now biracial, and it's still shifting.) In addition, many changes happen over the course of our lives which change the way we see ourselves: we graduate, we get married, we have kids, grandkids, and so on. It is important for young people to know that they are not the only ones who sometimes struggle with figuring out who they are and where they fit in . . . we all do from time to time, throughout our entire lives. We graduate from college and see ourselves as college grads, we take on a profession and become doctors or lawyers or editors, we get married and see ourselves as a husband or wife, we have children and take on the role of parent, our kids have kids and we become grandparents, and on and on.

In a study done by psychologists from Emory University, researchers found that the most important thing you can do for your family (as well as for corporate and military teams) is to develop a strong personal narrative.[2] Those families who knew more about their history (their narrative) exhibited a stronger sense of control over their lives, developed higher self-esteem, and could moderate the effects of stress better. Psychologists discovered that narratives tended to take one of three paths: ascending—we had nothing and worked our butts off; descending—we had it all and

---

[2] Jennifer G. Bohanek, Kelly A. Marin, Robyn Fivush, and Marshall P. Duke, "Family Narrative Interaction and Children's Sense of Self," *Family Process* 45, no. I (March 2006): 39–54.

lost it; and the most healthful narrative, oscillating—we had our ups and downs. Families and teams that have the most confidence are those that understand they belong to something bigger than themselves. Telling our stories reinforces how we are all connected in a universal way.

So how do I go about telling my story, or getting someone else to tell me theirs? Most people are not very adept at crafting a well-constructed personal story and then sharing that with another person (or in a group). Many people are shy or hesitant, and in some cultures the very idea of opening up to another person this way might carry risks or be considered taboo. And then, of course, there is the impediment of talking to someone you do not know or who does not look or sound like you. Different accents, ethnicities, skin shades, even traditional (or nontraditional) clothing can prohibit us from talking to others.

All these deterrents aside, we must take risks. We must learn about others, fear be damned! Start by asking a question, maybe inquiring as to a person's hobbies. I was once at an annual diversity summit for a huge multinational corporation and the CEO was giving an address to a roomful of employees from locations across the globe. Following his talk, he opened the floor for questions. Employees lined up behind microphones stationed throughout the massive hotel ballroom, ready to pose questions to their corporate leader. Before calling on the first person, he requested that each person who stepped to the microphone state their name, the location where they worked, and their department and position and tell the room a few of their hobbies outside of work. It was a simple request—the hobbies—but it allowed him to find out some small thing that each person had a passion for, and in many cases he was thus able to establish a common connection between himself and that person.

Ask questions and, more importantly, offer more than one-word answers. These details—hobbies, where we live and work, our names—are a significant part of who we are, our life story. Don't be afraid to ask in order to begin the conversation.

You cannot define me. I define myself. I cannot let anyone define who I am, *whether I'm gay, whether I'm black, whether I'm a writer, whether I'm this or that. This is my own responsibility—to define myself. And I am not a finished product: I am always in construction because I learn, I have experience, and I see the world.*

JAMES BALDWIN

TOOL

Tell your story.

Open up and listen. By sharing our personal stories we discover commonalities.

ACTION

Ask questions!

In order to get information or answers, we must be willing to ask questions.

STARTING POINTS

- Name three hobbies.
- What is your favorite way to spend your time?
- What is your favorite journey?
- What do you consider your greatest achievement?
- Who is your hero?

TWO

Don't Judge
the Differences

*If you see people as enemies or obstacles or traps, you will be
at constant war with them and with yourself. Whereas if you
choose to see people as puzzles, and you see yourself as a puzzle,
then you will be constantly delighted, because eventually, if you
dig deep enough into anybody, if you really look under the hood
of someone's life, you will find something familiar.*

NATHAN HILL

THE NIX

I was in the middle of a block of shows booked at central
Pennsylvania colleges in the middle of February, Black History
Month. I flew to Harrisburg, rented a car, and proceeded to
present shows within the Penn State system from Harrisburg to
York, Altoona, Berks, Schuylkill, Allegheny, Hazleton, Mont Alto,
Scranton, and Wilkes-Barre. I'd do a school at noon, then drive
to a different location for a show that night, for five days straight.
Some locations had theaters, others simply large rooms, and at one
place I used a classroom. There could be up to a couple hundred
people attending, but most audiences were in the twenty to forty
range, and on one occasion we nearly had to cancel when just five

came. Getting students to show up for what is billed as a "diversity lecture" is a tough sell. Add to that the concept of a one-man play, and many students have a difficult time trying to wrap their heads around the event.

The good news was that no matter how many were in the audience—five or a hundred and five—the response was always quite enthusiastic. People stayed and talked, asked questions, even at times asked for an autograph. They told their own stories, and some walked away in tears.

At one of the schools I arrived early for my noon presentation, having driven that morning from a town a couple hours away. After setting my props and getting ready for the show I had almost two hours to kill before students would be there. Since the performance space was near the cafeteria, I popped in to grab a salad . . . heavier meals are not something I can digest prior to such a workout.

While seated at a table eating my salad, a young man approached and asked if he could sit down. I of course obliged, and we struck up a conversation. He inquired if I was the speaker for the upcoming program, and I confirmed that I was indeed. He asked what I was going to speak about. My usual line is to simply say I am retelling the story about my quest to find my biological father. This seemed to intrigue him and he pressed for more information, but I suggested he'd be disappointed if I shared more since it would taint his experience of the play.

"A play?" he said inquisitively. "No one said anything about a play."

"Well," I said, "I am most often advertised as a speaker or lecturer but what I really do is perform a play about my own life journey."

"Wow, that sounds really interesting."

He told me he wasn't necessarily a big theatergoer but had been known to enjoy a play on occasion. He'd never seen a one-man play before, and when I told him I would be portraying more than a dozen different characters, he looked as if his head was about to explode.

"How do you do that?!" he asked incredulously.

"Very carefully," I joked.

We talked until the time for my presentation approached. He was quite engaged and engaging. When I got up to go start the show, he offered his help with anything I might need. Since my setup is pretty self-contained, I graciously declined and encouraged him to enjoy the show, saying that I would look forward to speaking to him after he'd seen it, and he said he looked forward to that conversation, too.

The cramped room was packed that afternoon with close to fifty students and faculty escaping the cold for their annual Black History Month event. The students seemed to be really entertained as well as surprised. At the point in the show when I reveal that my dad is Black—thus making me Black—there were audible gasps and laughs in the crowd. Afterward the Q&A was lively as students wanted to know more about the impact this journey had had on my life.

Following the Q&A, I offer a bit of a wrap-up, encourage people to follow me on social media or write to me, and thank them for coming out. As the program concludes and people head off to wherever they're going next, I am usually surrounded by a number of folks who want to ask more in-depth questions, offer their stories, or sometimes seek advice. As I stepped from the stage I noticed the young man with whom I had spent the hours before the show turn and head out of the room. Having spent so much time with him, making an indelible connection, I couldn't help but wonder if he'd found my discovery difficult to wrap his arms around. The young man had no doubt made some assumptions about whom he'd been talking to, and over the course of my show he may have discovered those assumptions were incorrect. Or it could have been that he didn't care for my play—was confused by it or found the presentation style not to his liking. But I suspected something deeper since we'd shared a great lunch together, and I'd anticipated continuing our conversation following my presentation. Something about my play or the story behind it disrupted the way he'd perceived me, causing him discomfort. We'd found so much in common during our pre-show dialogue, and now there was something different, causing him to flee.

✻ ✻ ✻ ✻

Then there is the story of—let's call him "Wayne"—a thirtysomething Asian American man who was the director of multicultural student activities at a college in Boston. Arriving early to the venue, I had an opportunity to chat with him briefly before my show, and after giving him a brief synopsis of my story, I asked him about his American experience. He told me he was brought up outside Boston by Chinese parents who felt it was most important for their children to assimilate into American society. His demeanor was very cheerful, and he seemed comfortable with what he described as a typical American upbringing, albeit in an Asian family. When I asked what was his first experience with race or racism, he couldn't think of anything, shrugging it off as if he'd never really experienced any problems. Slowly, however, he remembered that when he was a young hockey player (against stereotype), he was told by a White kid to go eat his fried rice. He laughed a bit and shook his head, remarking that he'd sort of filed that incident away, had thought of it only as a childish encounter. He then told me a story about raising his daughter—a child who more closely resembles his

White wife: when he went with his daughter to school one day to be the story reader, her classmates all assumed he was the father of an Asian boy in the class and couldn't understand how he could be the dad of his White-looking daughter.

* * * *

There are so many identifiers and biases, both conscious and not, that are keeping us from making these connections. Most are minuscule in the bigger picture, but they get in our way whether we are aware of it or not. *That person looks different than me, sounds different than me, comes from a different place than I do.* So what?! Why should the color of one's skin prevent people from getting to know one another? When we start with these differences, we are not giving ourselves room to grow, to explore, to make connections. We cut ourselves off, not only from others but from growth within ourselves . . . knowledge.

What if, instead of immediately judging these differences, we sought out commonalities? We have far more in common than different. If we flipped the mental script and consciously searched for those mutual interests first, then embraced the differences, we'd be far better off. After all, if we were all the same, life would be boring. We are such a contradiction: we actually love our differences but simultaneously want to fit in. We crave to discover and embrace the unique—the coolest watch, the most unique looking car, the wildest hairdo, the latest one-of-a-kind thing—while at the same time we vilify those who stand out too far from the mainstream. However, it's the differences that make us stand out as people and make corporations, services, and products unique in the marketplace.

Anthropologists tell us there are more differences within a race than between races. If that's true, what's keeping us apart? I suggest it is our fear of actually getting to know one another.

* * * *

At a public high school in Connecticut in early 2016 I found myself in an auditorium performing for close to 750 predominantly White students. As can be the case at some schools, it sometimes takes a good ten to fifteen minutes into the show before the students settle down, become used to the presentation style, and become engaged with the story. I don't present often at public schools as their financial resources for this type of programming are much more limited than at private institutions. There is also a noticeable difference between public and private audiences. With less money at their disposal, public schools have fewer opportunities for assemblies and even fewer chances to expose their students to theatrical presentations. For the most part, public school students are not subjected to the same kind of rigorous and disciplined atmosphere found in private schools, and therefore they can be slightly less respectful, more restless, and sometimes even annoying.

I always provide an introduction to be read just before the show starts in order to give the audience a few vital bits of information that can help put the performance into context. The most important thing they need to know is that the story is true. In the past I have used the term *autobiographical*, but sadly I have come to the realization that many people are unfamiliar with this word. I recently changed the wording to *true story* in an attempt to make things perfectly clear. There are two other important things about the introduction: first, the audience is not told my secret—the fact that as a White guy, I go on a journey and discover my Black roots, which for some might ruin the surprise; and second, they need to know that I portray a dozen different characters during the course of the show. This helps give the audience a sense of the form the show takes and allows them to follow along a little more easily.

So, following the introduction, which at this school was given by the principal (who had made clear to me in earlier conversations the importance of attempting to push a school-wide dialogue about race and identity), I began the show and quickly gained the attention of the entire auditorium. As always, there were a few students sleeping or surfing the internet on their phones, but the bulk were journeying along, unaware of where they were being led.

And as is typical, there were a few gasps and laughs when I reveal my dad's Black heritage and even more laughs as I portray what I consider to be a Black sense of self. Overall I remember them being a pretty great, responsive audience, unafraid to laugh at comedic moments and the sometimes eccentric characters. I commenced the post-show talkback, which had been my custom since about 2014, asking a couple questions of the audience. This had become a standard procedure over the last few years due to the kind of hypersensitivity I've noticed in many audiences of young people in high school and college settings. Let me elaborate on this hypersensitivity a moment and we'll come back to this story.

* * * *

There seems to be an oversensitivity toward anything that has a whiff of stereotypes, racism, or, as is now widely discussed, micro-inequities or microaggressions.[3] I first noticed this shift around the time of the Trayvon Martin incident, which took place in Sanford, Florida, in 2014. Following this was a slew of killings of unarmed Black men: Eric Garner, Freddie Gray, Michael Brown, Tamir Rice, Laquan McDonald, Walter Scott, John Crawford. One result was

---

[3] Micro-inequities refer to small subtle remarks, frequently unconscious, that devalue, discourage, and ultimately impair performance. It may include looks, gestures, tone of voice, nuance, inflection, inference, an absence of message, or actions that exclude individuals. Similarly, micro-aggressions are defined as everyday actions and behavior that have harmful effects on marginalized groups.

Black Lives Matter, followed by protests in St. Louis and Baltimore. Black people (along with others) were protesting the outrageous inequalities in policing and criminal justice, causing some White people—mostly those on the right side of the political spectrum—to push back. These incidents set the stage for campus unrest at the University of Missouri, Yale University, Ithaca College, and many others.

The offense at Missouri was that the administration had not been supportive of students of color when they complained repeatedly about racist incidents on campus. Over a period of years, a variety of situations had been reported to the president's office and apparently ignored. Students had had enough, and the Black students on the highly ranked football team threatened to boycott their next game unless the president stepped down. If you want to strike fear in the hearts of administrators, threatening them with the loss of hundreds of thousands of dollars of revenue due to a canceled game hits the school where it counts most.[4] The president did step down (I'm guessing with pressure from the board), a position was created for a director of diversity and inclusion, and the students were assured their voices and complaints would be heard. However, according to the *New York Times*, freshman enrollment had dropped by more than 35 percent (42 percent for Blacks, 21 percent for Whites) in the two years following these protests. Black enrollment

---

[4] Michael Pearson, "A Timeline of the University of Missouri Protests," CNN, November 10, 2015, https://www.cnn.com/2015/11/09/us/missouri-protest-timeline/index.html; Elahe Izadi, "The Incidents that Led to the University of Missouri President's Resignation," *Washington Post*, November 9, 2015, https://www.washingtonpost.com/news/grade-point/wp/2015/11/09/the-incidents-that-led-to-the-university-of-missouri-presidents-resignation/; John Elagon, "At University of Missouri, Black Students See a Campus Riven by Race," *New York Times*, November 11, 2015, https://www.nytimes.com/2015/11/12/us/university-of-missouri-protests.html.

overall fell from 10 percent to 6 percent in that time.[5] And, as had happened with the policing issue, White students began to push back on what Black students saw as inequities in their experience and education. It doesn't seem like the Black students' issues have been heard and understood.

Similar situations occurred at Ithaca College and other places, where students of color were demanding inclusion, setting off a chain of events that culminated in what I think has been a backlash of sensitivity. Schools that previously lacked a chief diversity officer were now creating this position on campus, along with an office of multicultural student affairs. Some even began to recognize what is referred to as cultural taxation, which the insufficient number of faculty members of color were experiencing. *Cultural taxation* is a term used to describe how faculty of color are sought out for help, guidance, support, and assistance by students of color, adding to each faculty member's already full plate of responsibilities.

In addition to students of color finding their voices on campuses, other groups were gaining their collective strength as well. LGBTQ students in particular were speaking out against a rash of bathroom laws being passed in states across the country, and corporations began backing up the LGBTQ community. Various groups of marginalized students were finding their voices, which was met with swift pushback from conservative-leaning student groups. Marginalized groups were demanding safe spaces be created on campuses for those who felt threatened and sought a place of refuge. These "snowflakes," so dubbed by conservative voices, were weak "babies" unable to stand up to the harsh realities of life.

---

5 Anemona Hartocollis, "Long after Protests, Students Shun the University of Missouri," *New York Times*, July 9, 2017, https://www.nytimes.com/2017/07/09/us/university-of-missouri-enrollment-protests-fall out.html.

In addition, conservative and White students suggested their voices were being squashed—seeing it as a sort of reverse racism.

Another sign of this increased sensitivity was students calling for trigger warnings for any campus-sponsored class or event. Trigger warnings are notices about course materials, lectures, or other classroom content that may be distressing to people who have experienced some form of psychological trauma, for example, racism, rape, homophobia, xenophobia, and so on. Student groups on some campuses pushed for warnings to be posted to allow traumatized students to opt out of certain classrooms or lectures. At some universities, invited speakers with controversial views have been disinvited or disrupted during their visits. Many comedians who used to tour campuses regularly have ceased accepting college engagements to avoid nasty confrontations and boycotts, which they see as an affront to free speech.

✵ ✵ ✵ ✵

I was unaware at the time but this sensitivity was about to crop up in my talkback that afternoon in Connecticut, much like experiences I've had at several high schools more recently. In an effort to diffuse this oversensitivity I had devised a set of questions which could open up a healthy conversation on issues that might be seen as offensive. I asked the audience that day, "By a show of hands, how many people felt the Black characters in the play were stereotypes?" On this day, as happens regularly when asking this question, a majority of the audience raised their hands. I then asked, "How many felt the White characters in the play were stereotypes?" and as per usual, a small fraction of the audience raised their hands.

This is a startling perception. Why would people see the Black characters more stereotypically than the White? And what are stereotypes? As defined in the dictionary, stereotypes are thoughts, beliefs, or attributes about a group of people without taking into consideration individual differences. Under that definition, we all have stereotypes that apply to us, whether we are Black, White, Asian, Hispanic, young, old, male, female, gay, Catholic, Jewish, Muslim, athletic, disabled, or whatever. There are stereotypes from each of the categories of which we are a part that apply to us. There are probably also an equal number or more of stereotypes from our respective categories that don't apply to us. However, most often we are being judged by the broad strokes of how we look and sound, sometimes consciously, most often unconsciously.

The way I portray my grandmother—a loud, large, southern Black woman—may appear to be stereotypical, but that does not mean she is a stereotype. She was an amazing cook but did not dance well; she was large but not lazy, constantly in motion doing something. Once we identify one or two traits as stereotypical, we unconsciously ascribe other traits of the stereotype, whether negative or positive, to that person. Both positive and negative stereotypes perpetuate a false story line. Not all Asians are good at math, nor are they all bad drivers.

The portrayals in my performance are further complicated by the fact that audience members are seeing only a very small fraction of these characters—literally one to two minutes total—but making judgments (mostly unconsciously) based on their own personal or impersonal experience with people like that. Therefore, those who have a family member similar to my granny might both see those traits as stereotypical *and* recognize that character as someone they know.

The characters are also deeply and unconsciously complicated because they are being portrayed by someone who looks like a White guy. We rarely see White people portray Black characters. Rare exceptions were Robert Downey Jr.'s portrayal of a racially resentful soldier in *Tropic Thunder* (assisted by the generous use of what might be considered blackface makeup, so overtly offensive that not a peep was heard regarding its merits) and the subtly suggestive, racially ambiguous drug dealer and pimp portrayed by Gary Oldman in *True Romance*. If my skin were a darker shade, more than likely a good number of people would perceive the Black characters in my play differently. (I am also portraying female characters, which likely affects the way some people perceive those characters.) If a Black man were portraying these characters, the response would certainly be different for both Blacks and Whites.

My characters are based on real people, and I have meticulously tried to portray them with as much authenticity as possible. Although several of my Black relatives—my grandmother, grandfather, and a cousin—never got an opportunity to see the show, others who knew them intimately have attended and can attest to this authenticity. And really, why would I stereotype my family? Wouldn't that be terribly disrespectful? If I can't play these characters in my family, Black and White, then who can? Who has permission to play my family? John Leguizamo has spoken frequently about the pushback he has received from Latin American audiences over what they perceive to be racist negative stereotypes in the portrayal of his family members. Tyler Perry has also commented on this phenomenon. Yet Puerto Rican and Colombian audiences *love* Leguizamo's one-man shows, and Tyler Perry's movies sell extraordinarily well in the Black community (although it appears he is putting his character Medea to sleep after all these years!).

Following the discussion at the high school that day, I opened the floor to questions, and there were a variety of thoughtful inquiries. Students wanted to know which box I now check on application forms (a frequent query), what kind of response my family had to the play—both Black and White—and whether I am closer to one side or the other. Near the end of the session we had time for one more question, which I fielded from a White teacher who was stationed at the back of the auditorium. He asked if I had performed the show for all-Black audiences and what their response was like. It seemed as if he'd been put up to this question by a group of Black students in his vicinity, and I just assumed they were too inhibited to ask the question.

I responded that I'd performed the show many times for predominantly Black audiences and the reception had been great. However, instead of elaborating on that, I wanted to delve back into identity, a topic that had come up earlier during the Q&A, so I mentioned a show I'd done at an all-Black church in the Bahamas. I told them that I had walked away with a very valuable lesson that day after presenting to a very appreciative audience. As is common, we'd had an extremely engaging post-show dialogue during which I noticed a small Black boy with his hand raised. I guessed his age at about eight or so, and when I called upon him he asked, "What is an African American?"

As I reported to my audience in Connecticut, at first I was confused about why he asked what seemed to be an easily answerable question. However, it came to me suddenly as to why he didn't understand: he was a Bahamian, that was his identity, not African. But if he came to America, he would be labeled an African American. I had used that term in the show and during the post-show dialogue, and the little boy was curious as to how it might apply to him. We Americans would force him to change his identity, or at the very least we would impose an identity on him that was not how he saw himself. This had been a very powerful moment and revelation for me, as I explained to the high school audience.

We wrapped up the Q&A, and as students streamed out of the auditorium, several stopped by the stage to ask me more personal questions, to thank me, or to tell me their own stories about identity. Two large, imposing boys, one Black, one White, couldn't understand why so many audience members thought the characters were stereotypes. The Black boy declared the characters were exactly like members of his own family and he found them both funny and loving.

Suddenly I was pulled aside by the principal, who'd been hovering about the stage. She asked me in a hushed and urgent voice if I could stick around and talk with some students in her office. I said of course, and she mentioned that there was a group of students of color who were quite upset by the show. Apparently a few even walked out during the performance. She wanted to gather us all in a conference room and discuss what had set them off.

The shift in this story—how it played out and what it reveals about the way in which we communicate about race—applies more directly to a different lesson I learned, so I will pick this story line up again in the next chapter.

✻ ✻ ✻ ✻

I did a presentation for a government agency, and afterward, following the dialogue with the audience, I was once again surprised at what a variety of people were affected by my story. Immediately following the play and dialogue I am usually approached by audience members who wish to thank me and who desire to ask for my advice on their own personal journeys. On this day, as I was speaking to several people, out of the corner of my eye I noticed a woman standing off to the side awaiting a chance to speak with me. First I spoke briefly with a White man who looked as if he could have been Grizzly Adams. He was a huge barrel of a guy sporting a massive beard and shaggy hair. As he stepped forward cautiously, his physical presence betrayed the peaceful way he approached. He struggled to form words, let alone a sentence, then settled on a simple, gentle thank you. As I shook his hand, he leaned in, embracing me in a big bear hug. Holding on perhaps slightly too long, I knew he'd been deeply affected by the show. As he stepped away, again thanking me, I could see tears welling up in his eyes.

When I turned to connect with the next person, it was the woman I had noticed earlier. I immediately recognized her as a person in transition, a trans woman, who quite obviously had been tearing as well. She reached out delicately extending her hand, then thanked me for sharing her story.

"Well, it's not really my story, but it is. I have struggled for years to find who I am and to finally embrace it . . . and it has not been easy," she said as she brushed the hair from her face. "I want to tell my story, like you, but maybe in a podcast. Can you tell me how I can do a podcast?"

I was still trying to wrap my head around her connection to my story when she began to tell me the details of her journey. She'd been in agony for years she said, struggling with wave after wave of inner confusion. As the conflict became more pronounced, she also became more clear as to who she really was and yet equally distressed by the fear of how to embrace it in a world that didn't. She became lost in what she described as "a river of alcohol," hoping that would lessen her pain.

Finally, one night she drank herself into oblivion and returned home to burn all her male clothing. She awoke the next morning, bleary-eyed but determined, and outfitted herself in the way she felt most comfortable, as a woman. Needless to say, her colleagues at work were unprepared and unaccepting of her transition. She was shunned and eventually fired. Somehow she had made her way to this government agency and got hired. There was no attempt on her part to hide her past, and her colleagues for the most part had been accepting and supportive.

As she shared this heartbreaking story of coming out, I noticed folks from the Diversity and Inclusion Department hovering around us, spellbound by her story. She thanked me again for "sharing such a brave story" and reiterated how it had forced her to look at her own journey of self and identity and how she thought it might make for a great podcast, asking again how she might go about producing such a thing. As I am a live performer, I had little I could share regarding her quest, aside from contacting her local National Public Radio station, where many podcasts originate. We hugged, I wished her luck on her journey, and the D&I folks swooped in to talk with her, perhaps unaware she'd been in their midst all along.

The beauty of her story, her struggle, her presence, was so uplifting. Like all of us trying to figure out who we are, where we fit in, she felt like an outsider. Despite what she knew was going to be a difficult transition for both her and others, she was determined to embrace her reality. These are the realities we must come to grips with . . . realities that don't always align with our view of the world. As much as we'd like to believe that we see and understand a great deal of the world around us, our thoughts and beliefs are significantly shaped by our circumstances and position. This lens through which we observe the world forms the way in which we do and do not perceive various people, places, and ideas.

* * * *

In the middle of January I had a booking at a small college in the far western part of North Dakota near the border with Montana. I flew to the nearest airport and then drove two hours through wind and blowing ice in subzero temperatures. The entire time I was thinking about two things: First, how many students would show up to a diversity lecture on a tiny campus in the middle of an ice storm? And second, how few students of color will there be on this middle-of-the-prairie campus? Oh, and I believe I was also thinking about the movie *Fargo* with the drive through the frozen tundra!

When I arrived, I made my way into the student center on campus, which to my surprise was buzzing with students . . . many of them of color! There was color everywhere, and it wasn't merely a handful like at most universities I had visited. I found the makeshift auditorium—basically a hotel ballroom with risers for a stage—and set up for my performance. As the presentation hour approached, I watched from behind a freestanding curtain as students poured into the cavernous room. An unexpected full house, perhaps as many as 350, of multicolored people!

The presentation went well, and the students responded without restraint, laughing in all the right places as I guided them along my personal journey. The post-show talkback included several great questions about identity and race: Did my newfound discovery alter the way I now saw racial relations? What had been my feelings about race prior to my discovery? What kind of advice could I offer to help people talk about race? Someone even asked if the message of diversity and inclusion was one of a political nature (more on that later).

Afterward, a group of Black students approached me and asked if they could take me to dinner—a first!—and have a conversation. I of course obliged, and the eight of us—myself, six Black students and one White—wound up at a Chili's that was still open at eight o'clock on a weeknight in this tiny college town.

During the conversation I discovered most of these students were on the school's much lauded track team (including the White student) and felt a deep disrespect by school administrators. Most had been brought there on scholarship from the islands of Jamaica, Bermuda, or the Bahamas, recruited for their outstanding talents in track and field. Their team was one of the top in the country but lacked basic things like shoes and other equipment. Yet the football team—which played in a lower NCAA division and was not highly ranked—had received all kinds of benefits and equipment. These track stars were forced to raise money personally for the necessary equipment to compete. They resented being the students who brought national attention to their school but completely ignored by the school when it came to the needs their sport demanded. This disparity in support was exacerbated by the fact that the team was almost entirely Black, and the football team was quite the opposite.

During our conversation the White student opened up to talk about her transition from a small all-White town located in the sticks of North Dakota. She'd never met a Black person before coming to this school and really had no idea of what to expect. She now found herself competing alongside Black students she had become quite close with over the year. She laughed about how some of the things she'd heard about Black people—they're loud, talk funny, are lazy, eat weird foods, and so on—could have easily been said about White people she knew. She learned, as she shared in front of all at the table that night, not to judge the differences.

I have been asked a few times—as I was by a student on this frigid campus that evening—if my message is one of a political nature. What makes a message of diversity and inclusion one about political ideology? The even bigger question is why are our politics so entwined with race, racism, and discrimination? What if, instead of viewing this from a political perspective, we saw this as a human issue? We're all human, right? We all need many of the same things? Many of us even desire some of the same things. It is a fact that we have more commonalities than differences. Why do we accentuate the differences?

Although there may be a kernel of truth in some of the fear-based dog whistles we hear, actual statistics do not support their cries. Immigrants are not committing crimes in greater numbers—facts show they commit proportionally less crime. Neither are Black people committing more crime—again, factual numbers show that Whites have both greater numbers for drug use and lower arrest and incarceration rates. Gay people are not recruiting our youth nor destroying the family unit; Catholic priests, however, are being exposed for their role in decades of sexual abuse. And perhaps even more twisted is the fact that domestic terrorism—White nationalism—is happening at much higher levels than what we're told takes place at the hands of radical Islam.

For the White people who inquire (in my experience, it has been Whites exclusively doing the asking) and those who fear the word *diversity* is a dog whistle hinting subtly at their perceived racism, I suggest looking up the definition. *Diverse* means variety, or different from each other. If White people are absent, then we are missing a component of a complete variety. Therefore, White is included in that definition, and Whites must be a part of this conversation. Without White, we are not diverse. When we begin to pass judgment unconsciously on the differences, we are consciously contributing to disharmony.

* * * *

Let me end this chapter with a story about style.

The day after the opening of my play at the Missouri Repertory Theatre I was walking down the street with a friend who had flown all the way from Oregon to see the play. It was my first day off since being in Kansas City, and my friend Mary and I had just shared a lovely lunch at a local café. I'd met Mary recently at a spiritual psychological retreat I had attended that summer. A slender woman with graying hair and a beaming smile, she embodied what I would call a full spirit. She was one of my instructors at the retreat and literally radiated with a glow of loving-kindness. She became fascinated with my story and was interested in how I had turned my life story into a one-man play. Intrigued, she'd decided to fly to Kansas City to attend the opening.

During lunch she inquired about various identity-related issues not fully explored in the context of the play. As we walked down the quaint street lined with boutiques following our lunch, she peppered me with questions: Had I suspected prior to my discovery that I might be black? Were there any signs or clues that might have been present which perhaps I had overlooked? Did friends suspect? How did others see me? As we walked and I tried to answer her questions to the best of my ability, I noticed out of the corner of my eye two African American men standing on the corner conversing. We approached the corner, and as if on cue, the one brutha who'd been keeping his eye on me raised his voice and said, "Brutha? . . . brutha?! . . . I'm talkin' t'you, my brutha."

I turned and said, "Hey, wha'sup?" in my best brotherly vernacular.

"Brutha, you got style, you know? You got class. The way you dress, the way you look, the way you carry yo'self . . . damn brutha, you lookin' good."

Smiling ear to ear and with a blushing tell-all face, I glanced over at my friend, her jaw now firmly on the ground. I turned back to the man and said, as nonchalantly as I could muster, "Thanks, brutha, I 'preciate the love," slapping hands in that all too common brotherly way.

As a dazed Mary and I continued down the street, she shook her head, smiled, and said, "I guess that answers my questions, doesn't it?"

So where does one start? First, I suggest everyone get out of their comfort zones (more on that later) and reach out to someone, meet someone, speak to someone who is not like you. It is safe to stay in our bubble, but philosophers from Roman to present time all expound on the merits of taking risks and how those can take us to new levels of knowledge, understanding, and humanity. Open up and say something, find something you have in common, then get curious about the differences.

Nothing is exciting if you know what the outcome is going to be.
JOSEPH CAMPBELL
THE HERO WITH A THOUSAND FACES

TOOL

Don't judge the differences.

Flip the script: instead of allowing the differences to create a wall between us, start by finding a mutual interest, then embrace the differences—after all, if we were all the same, we'd be bored! It's the differences that make us stand out as people, and it's the differences that make us unique in the marketplace.

ACTION

Ask *more* questions!

STARTING POINTS

- How did you come to do (or study) what you do (or study)? What made you interested in the work you do (or the things you are studying)?
- What interests do you have outside of work (school)?
- What kinds of hobbies do you have? (see chapter 1)

In these simple questions you can almost instantly find commonalities. Even if you don't share the same interests or hobbies, you may know someone who does, or you may learn something fascinating about a person that would provoke you to ask more questions. For example, if someone's hobby is beekeeping, I don't know about you, but I would want to know more about that!

And here are some questions that can be used to find both commonalities and differences to embrace:

- Who had a great influence on you when you were young?
- Who is the most influential person in your life now and why? What effect have they had on you?
- What life event has had the greatest impact on you and why?
- Have you ever had an "Ah ha" moment in your life? Tell me about it.
- What are you afraid of, something that you are either embarrassed about or have never told anyone?
- What are you very grateful for?

THREE

Recognize There Isn't One Way to Have a Conversation about Race

Trump recently said he has a great relationship with the Blacks, although unless the Blacks are a family of White people, I think he's mistaken.

SETH MEYERS

AT THE WHITE HOUSE CORRESPONDENTS' DINNER, 2011

Back in 2012, community organizations in Duluth, Minnesota, decided they wanted to launch a campaign to raise awareness about racial issues in a town that was over 90 percent White and to start conversations around those issues. They dubbed it the Unfair Campaign, and the initial goal was to draw attention to the overwhelming Whiteness in town. They came up with several different ideas, which were placed on billboards across town. The billboards not only raised community members' awareness but angered a good number of White people in town. One of the billboards read:

IT'S HARD TO SEE RACISM WHEN YOU'RE WHITE

scrawled across the faces of White men and women.

Needless to say, the reaction from many leaning right—FOX News in particular—was swift. They thought it was divisive and . . . wait for it, racist! Critics felt the message stereotyped Whites, was essentially negative, biased, and/or accusatory. Did anyone really bother to *read* the message? It didn't say:

WHITE PEOPLE ARE RACIST

It didn't even have the word *all* in it. At its most blatant it was *suggesting* that White people have difficulties seeing racism. *Racism*: prejudice and discrimination based on the belief that one's race is superior to another. To this I will add the concept of unconscious bias: prejudices we hold of which we are unaware or unconscious. The problem of White privilege is that Whites moving through a world that is predominantly White can't see their privilege. We don't see racism because it is not a part of our experience (I'm both White and Black, but to most people I project mainly as a White man). If it is not a part of our experience, we tend to be blind to its effects. The authors of the campaign were not suggesting *all* White people are racist, nor most White people, nor specific White people. They were merely suggesting that as White, it can be more difficult to put oneself in a Black (gay, Muslim, Hispanic, etc.) person's shoes and see or experience what they do.

Many folks in the Duluth community found that campaign insightful and helpful. They were open and willing to take a look at what it truly meant to stand in someone else's shoes. There were others who thought it offensive and accusatory. They felt as though they were being identified as racist, prejudiced. These folks didn't see the need to talk and felt there'd been too much emphasis on race.

Similarly the Black Lives Matter movement has been vilified for what is perceived as its militancy, not to mention its supposed exclusion of Whites. Critics claim this group to be violent, extremist, and all manner of exclusionary. These same critics haven't really bothered to talk to Black Lives Matter members to discover what they think and have sometimes misconstrued what the movement is all about. Critics tend to rely on information from like-minded people. This is what is referred to as confirmation bias: we seek to confirm biases and beliefs we already hold by obtaining information from sources that verify it. Like the Unfair Campaign in Duluth, the movement is not titled Only Black Lives Matter. Some have suggested it might help if the title was Black Lives Matter Too. Are White people so insecure they need to have that spelled out?

* * * *

The conversation about differences is difficult, messy, and uncomfortable. There are so many different and challenging reactions when people are asked to talk about race. Some suggest we talk about it too much, others are afraid to discuss, some are exasperated, some angry, and some are opinionated and act as if theirs is the one and only opinion that matters.

The truth is that there isn't any one way to have a conversation about race and identity. If there was one way to talk about it, don't you think we'd all be doing it in order to avoid feeling the discomfort, anger, and confusion? As I mentioned in the opening chapter, the discussion about race and identity is not formulaic, it isn't math or science that has proven theorems. It is emotional and personal. We each have a different experience with race and identity, and we bring these differing unique understandings to the conversation. That can make for wildly different assumptions about how we should collectively perceive the situation. What is lost is that there isn't one collective experience of race; there's no one Black experience just as there isn't any one White experience. I am not saying that White people don't benefit from the privilege of having light or white skin. Some Whites may recognize this, but it seems most do not. Many are challenged to think of a remedy, while others find the idea of White privilege preposterous. It all depends on what lens we view the world through . . . and some might suggest here that my lens is cracked!

Let's return here to the story from the last chapter about the high school in Connecticut. We left off at the point where I was pulled aside by the principal and informed about a group of students who took offense to my presentation, and I was asked to stay and speak with them. I quickly gathered my belongings and was rushed to the conference room in anticipation of what had been foreshadowed as a confrontation, and awaited the students' arrival. Just as I arrived, the teacher who had posed the last question about performing my show for Black audiences came racing in to inform us that a group of Black students were in the cafeteria and were so offended they refused to talk. I said I would be happy to meet with the group of offended Black students in the cafeteria, but they had told the teacher that they would leave if I tried to enter their safe space. There was a great deal of consternation about what to do and how to handle the situation, and it was suggested that the teacher go back and plead with them once again. He left, and the principal, a couple teachers, and I discussed what might have taken place to create the students' displeasure. One suggestion was that they had become offended by what they perceived as offensive racist stereotypes, even though they'd been told it was a true story and I had led a dialogue about stereotypes following the show. I learned that some of these students may not have actually heard the introduction and therefore may not have realized it was a true story.

When the teacher returned, we were informed that one student had agreed to speak with us, a Hispanic boy. We were happy the teacher had prevailed and awaited the young man's arrival. While we waited, I was told this was an exceptional kid who also had a deep interest and involvement in theater. When he arrived and we'd dispensed with greetings, I realized how intimidating the room might seem to him with five administrators or faculty members and one student, and with no people of color other than myself and the student. We thanked him for agreeing to join and tried to assure him that we wanted to hear his unvarnished opinion, and those of his friends. He was hesitant at first but gradually opened up as I tried to steer the conversation so that it was mostly between him and me.

He told me he and his friends were offended by the racist stereotypes. When I asked what stereotypes specifically he said, "Well when you pulled out that African statue and started dancing, we were like, nah, he didn't just do that, did he?!"

"Let me ask you," I countered, "in that moment of my story, did you think I hung up the phone with my father, and, after discovering he was Black, I just suddenly pulled out an African statue . . . from . . . where? Out of . . . what, my closet? And then mysteriously James Brown music descended from the sky?"

He thought a moment, then replied carefully, "No, not really, but that don't make those things less racist."

"Let me ask you what makes someone Black, aside from the color of their skin, perhaps? What makes you what you are? What are you, if you don't mind me asking?"

"I'm Puerto Rican and Black."

"So which is it . . . Puerto Rican or Black?"

"I'm both."

"Aside from your friends and family, who knows that?"

"I'm not sure I understand . . ."

"If you hadn't told me, which you hadn't, wouldn't I be left to guess based on what I see?"

"I guess."

"And if you are both, do all people who are Puerto Rican and Black identify as both . . . or do some identify as Black and some Puerto Rican?"

"I guess some say one, and some say the other."

"And what makes you Black, or Puerto Rican, or both?"

"What do you mean?" he asked, now fully engaged in the debate.

"Well, is it the color of your skin? The music you listen or dance to? The clothes you wear? The food you eat? What is it that makes you who you are?"

"Well, it's a lot of things—music, food, clothes, family . . ."

"For you . . . and for others it might be different."

"Yeah, that makes sense."

"So what I am trying to do by pulling out that statue is force you, the audience, to think about what makes us who we are. What makes someone . . . *me* . . . Black? I am using what is called a theatrical device—the statue suddenly appearing, the music blasting on, the dance, the joke about college applications—to push the idea and question what makes someone Black. These things are stereotypical to many people, so I am forcing the audience to confront that and think about what might be distinctly Black cultural signposts. Does that make sense?"

"Okay, yeah, I can kinda see that, but what about the accents, the characters . . . they all seem pretty big, over the top."

"If I had darker skin, do you think they would have seemed more real, more lifelike to you?"

"Maybe."

"And do you or any of your friends have characters like that in your families?"

"I suppose I do."

"We all do . . . even White people have 'characters' in their families. As I said during the talkback, we all have stereotypes that apply to us and originate from the multiple categories we are a part of. Whether we are male or female, young or old, Black, White, Asian, or Hispanic, there are a few stereotypes from those various categories that apply to us . . . not all of them, but a few might be spot on."

"Yeah, sure . . . I get that. I see what you are saying . . . makes more sense now."

And with that we smiled and shook hands. As I left the school I couldn't help but think about how the issue of race—and how we go about talking about it or not—is fraught from both sides. White people, as I mentioned earlier, are often afraid and have very little experience engaging in what they see as a very uncomfortable conversation. Yet people of color can become so offended and entrenched—as a result of the pain they've had to endure and the hurt of racist stereotypes and dog whistles—that they refuse to participate. This deep polarization prohibits us from really making any progress when it comes to understanding one another's experience of race.

✻ ✻ ✻ ✻

Sometimes even those tasked with the job of diversity and inclusion have a difficult time figuring out how to approach the conversation.

About seven years ago I remember reading about an all-girls college in the East that had been experiencing repeated racial incidents over the course of a couple months. I tried contacting people within the administration and faculty numerous times, hoping to talk to them about how my story and work might help create a space for dialogue on their campus. My office sent promotional materials explaining my methods, emphasizing the safe, nonthreatening aspects of the program. Included in these packets were always letters of recommendation from similar schools, along with a long list of past presentations and clients. I tried calling a few times but was never able to get anyone to call me back.

Then a few years later, I was offered a booking at a private preparatory high school across the street from this college. Oddly, it just so happened that this prep school actually shared the college's auditorium when hosting events. And if that wasn't coincidence enough, in the weeks leading up to my visit, the college had another breaking story on national news about a racial situation on campus involving Confederate flags hung in the windows of a dorm room on campus.

It had been several years since I last reached out to them, but I thought I would try once again to contact the diversity person on this college campus and invite them to drop by their own auditorium in a few weeks to witness my presentation. This time I actually got the diversity administrator on the phone, and I tried to be as cheery as I could, seeing as how her circumstances might not be quite so bright at the moment. She greeted me rudely and was cold and immediately dismissive. I tried to brush that aside and mentioned I was actually going to be on her campus giving a presentation. She became tongue-tied and seemed flummoxed as to what to say to me. Stumbling over her words, she quickly said she could not come to the presentation. I suggested that it was harmless and that I was not implying that she "purchase" my service but merely attend a presentation she might find interesting and enlightening. She claimed she had a meeting that morning with her committee, and when I suggested that perhaps they all might want to attend as a way to expand their conversation, she declined and briskly ended the call. It seemed clear that she felt she knew what she was doing on campus with regard to racial incidents and needed no further help or ideas, although it was obvious these incidents formed a repeating pattern. I was kind on the phone, did not try to give her a hard sell on my services, and simply suggested there might be something to glean for her own personal and professional purposes. It certainly couldn't have been more convenient for her committee to attend! Alas, she was barely able to speak to me, let alone find the time to attend a program that could have been beneficial to her predicament.

✵ ✵ ✵ ✵

As I slowly ventured into the corporate diversity and inclusion (D&I) space, I was giddy at being asked to present to some of the highest-profile companies. I was also somewhat intimidated by the enormous leap I anticipated I would need in the knowledge and skills to make this transition. I quickly discovered that there are perhaps hundreds of companies providing diversity and inclusion training to the multinational world of corporations and government agencies. Many of these people have years of experience and training, and some come loaded with degrees and additional educational certificates. I held a bachelor of fine arts degree in theater from the University of Minnesota and had started theater businesses, worked independently as an actor and writer, and had a decorative painting contracting business to fill in the gaps when things in the entertainment world were tight. I was certainly not certified in any kind of D&I training, nor did I know much about the field until I suddenly found myself deep in the middle of it. Although it took some time to go from that first set of presentations for a corporation outside of Philadelphia to my next corporate gig, once things started rolling, the corporate world really opened up to what I was sharing and understood deeply the need for dialogue.

During this transition, it was important for me to learn as much as I could about the D&I space, as well as arm myself with as much knowledge about the issues as I could gather in order to facilitate meaningful and relevant post-show conversations. If I were going to be viewed as an expert, I was going to need to digest as much expertise as I could.

I began reading everything I could get my hands on that dealt with the wide range of issues surrounding race, identity, diversity, inclusion, gender, sexual orientation, age, and disability. Having read a good deal of James Baldwin in college, along with most of W. E. B. Du Bois's seminal book, *The Souls of Black Folk*, I found my way to Beverly Tatum's *Why Are All the Black Kids Sitting Together in the Cafeteria?*, a wealth of information and practice. This was just the beginning of my still ongoing journey with the written word about identity (see Bibliography at the end of the book). I also scoured the internet using RSS feeds to gather articles that had anything to do with these topics. Utilizing this treasure of information, I was able to push the post-show conversations in ever-widening directions that had relevance to my own story, making connections to my specific story wherever possible, and at the same time helping audience members see the universal experience in our personal stories.

As I began to dialogue with people, listening to their stories and facilitating often awkward discussions about these delicate and contentious issues, I experienced all manner of crazy, enlightening, provocative, and deeply moving responses from audience members. What became clear quite early on was the fact that our shared experiences connected us all in sometimes obvious, sometimes obscure ways. I wouldn't necessarily say themes emerged, but the general resistance to having conversations that centered around issues of race was prevalent almost everywhere I went, whether it was high schools, colleges, or later in corporations and government agencies.

The other important common thread in my research: there wasn't any one way people went about talking about or discussing race and identity, just as there wasn't one way in which D&I facilitators approached the work. Although the terminology may have been the same, the methods varied. The D&I world is filled with talk about unconscious bias (or implicit bias), microinequities, cultural competency, intersectionality, and the like. How facilitators get participants to discover and uncover these ideas varies immensely, and measuring the impact of their programs can be challenging. Thus there are some people who feel D&I programs and training have mixed results and others who feel these programs are ridiculous. They see the growth of the D&I industry as a waste of corporate time and money. Many of these folks tend to be the same people who, when asked to attend a diversity event (or training), wave it off as something that doesn't have anything to do with them. That kind of thing is for Black or gay people, is often their response. Or they ask why this type of training is necessary, what do you hope to accomplish? I can't tell you how many times I have been asked to present as a keynote for a diversity conference and, as I look out at the audience I see the room filled with women, people of color, and people with disabilities. I mentioned this earlier, but if the definition of *diversity* means "a compilation of differing elements" or "a variety," then it is important for us to recognize that if one group feels this doesn't apply to them, then as a whole we aren't actually diverse.

✳ ✳ ✳ ✳

During the winter of 2016 I was asked to do a presentation at a high school in Ferguson, Missouri. It was to be sponsored by a large corporation with local headquarters where I was performing and would be made available to the school free of charge. I was excited about the possibility of performing in a school that was the epicenter of the flashpoint that resulted after the death of a young Black teen by the name of Michael Brown at the hands of a police officer. I was also a bit nervous as to what I was walking into: What kind of school is it? How would they respond? What is the goal?

Once the dates and times were confirmed I received a message from the principal asking if I would be amenable to working with the school's press person. I responded in the affirmative and said that although I was traveling a great deal, I would be more than happy to make time to speak to any media people. Two weeks passed and I didn't hear a word so I reached out and offered some days and times I could potentially make myself available to speak to media. The principal got back to me and said the school suddenly found themselves working between two different press people, so he wasn't sure anything was going to happen. It sounded strange to me, but I had an alternative idea.

I had previously worked quite successfully with a publicist out of New York, who had some terrific contacts in the media, so I suggested she might be able to help and I said I would cover the cost. I suddenly got emails from both the principal and an agent of the corporation (who was sponsoring this visit) saying we urgently needed to have a conference call regarding this situation.

I put together a call with all the parties: my publicist, the school principal, my corporate contact, and the corporation's director of communications. For the first time, they expressed fears of the media dredging up the difficulties in the community as a result of the killing of Michael Brown and subsequent protests in Ferguson. The publicist and I suggested we could talk to media outlets and pitch them on my story, focusing on the dramatic form of the presentation and how it was being brought to schools for Black History Month. We had hoped this would allay their fears by putting the emphasis where we felt it belonged, on my unique and powerful story.

They offered their unenthusiastic approval for our direction but adamantly refused to participate or allow any of the students to be a part of these efforts. Both myself and my publicist were taken aback, since it was the principal who had originally suggested getting the media involved. As we dug into the reasons for their sudden hesitation, we discovered the principal was a White man who was leading a predominantly Black school. This dynamic was similar to that of the mostly White police force in the city, which so many people of color had complained about. The principal shared he was worried about agitating a deep wound in their community and was determined to "protect" his students. The communications director agreed and added that now was not the time to have a conversation about race while smoldering anger was still present.

This left me confused as to why the corporation was even interested in sponsoring my visit in the first place, and what it was they—both the principal and the corporation—expected of my visit. It felt like a continuation of repeated national attempts to forge dialogue about guns following mass shootings, only to be shut down with the same line: *Now is not the time.* I tried to point out this inconsistency to the principal and communications director but was met with silence on the line. "It's 2016, if we don't feel comfortable talking about race now, then when do you think we will?" Silence.

The presentation at the school turned out to be rather unremarkable. The group of students selected to attend were not prepared in any way for what they were seeing. The entirely Black audience of approximately seventy-five was unaccustomed to seeing theater, they were not encouraged to be a respectful audience, and they were scattered throughout a large auditorium (approximately 600 seats). Most of the students seemed bored or at least unable to truly comprehend why they were in attendance. Some of the students talked audibly throughout the show, and not one of the teachers—whom I could make out at the corners of the auditorium—did anything to quiet them. In situations like this in the past I have stopped the show and called for those who are disruptive to leave. It's a fine line, and I have to find a point in the show where it makes sense to stop and where I will be able to pick it back up easily. But each time I got to a place where it would make sense to stop, the audience was quiet. At the time, it seemed to make more sense to continue rather than disrupt the program. Retrospectively, I think I should have stopped and asked people to either quiet down or leave.

During the talkback, however, most of the students were quite engaged, asking questions about what it felt like growing up thinking I was White, then discovering I am Black. Had I ever acted in racist ways toward people when I was younger, and if not, how did I react when I experienced those who did? Many of the questions were well thought out and seemed to arise from having paid close attention to the story, which had not been my experience of this audience. Why hadn't my Black family come to look for me? Your dad seems very light-skinned; did that affect the way he and his family fit into the community? Have you had a reunion of your Black and White families, and if so, what was that like? Overall, aside from doing a few radio interviews, the entire fiasco felt like a wasted opportunity for students, the school staff, the corporate sponsor, and, of course, for myself. Although the students seemed disinterested or perhaps distracted during the presentation, their involvement and engagement afterward was robust. The administration on the other hand, had not prepared the students, took no actions to help guide them through the event, and seemed to have little interest in any kind of follow-up. Why bother?!

* * * *

I am reminded of a time early on in my journey when a similar conversation took place among an all-Black group of audience members with a very different result.

An African American couple had attended the opening of my show at the Missouri Repertory Theater and were so deeply moved that they invited a rather large group of friends to return with them toward the end of the run. The couple also decided to throw a party at their house following that last performance and asked me to be the guest of honor with their friends who had just seen the show.

I was dropped off at their house by a staff member from the theater. I remember it being in a rather tony neighborhood with long driveways and winding stairs leading up to regal entrances with broad dense doorways. As the door swung open, I was greeted by my hostess, whom I had met previously, a warm darker-skinned woman with twinkling eyes and a glimmering smile. She was gracious and delighted by my presence as she welcomed me into an enormous foyer complete with a massive curving grand staircase and an immense crystal chandelier. As she escorted me toward their substantial dining room, the place was aflutter with tuxedo-clad staff refilling drinks and passing hors d'oeuvres among the well-dressed Black guests gathered. As we made our way into the grand dining room, guests began to applaud. It was quite a sensation to be feted in that manner, but I was truly unprepared for this type of reception.

They'd set up a comfortable bar stool for me in one corner of the grand room while the guests, consisting entirely of Black folks, gathered around, eating and drinking. The situation felt odd for an number of reasons, not the least of which I was sitting among what appeared to be members of the Black upper class of Kansas City. It was remarkable first and foremost that I was in a room full of Black folks, and then, of course, the implication that these were perhaps some of KC's talented tenth.[6] I had the awkward feeling of being

_____

[6] It was W. E. B. Du Bois who affectionately referred to a Black leadership class in his essay "The Talented Tenth," published in a book of essays by leading Black intellectuals; Booker T. Washington, ed., *The Negro Problem* (New York: J. Pott and Co., 1903).

on display, and yet I was treated like a guest of honor. One by one folks began to express their sincere appreciation for the play, the courage it took to tell my story, and the way in which it challenged people to think when they left the theater.

People shared personal stories of colorism and passing within their own Black families—the hardships and discriminations that happen between light- and dark-skinned Black folk. There was talk about the Inkwell, the famous beach on Martha's Vineyard, which had been a vacation spot for many affluent Black families. We discussed soul food and music, along with other culturally Black cultural signposts. We even had a dialogue about the N-word—its use and abuse and the difference between *niggers* and *nigga's*. It was an eye-opening experience that cemented for me what had become a pattern: people of all races seemed to relate quite profoundly to the story, provoking in them all a need to talk about difficult issues. It helped me recognize that even among Black people, there were different ways in which people approached and talked about the topics of race and identity.

*   *   *   *

We all have different experiences with race and identity and therefore bring different points of view to the table—this is actually the strength of our collective spirit, our diversity. This should probably be the first thing discussed when embarking on a conversation about race and identity (especially in mixed company). Acknowledge this up front with a person or group when a topic of race or identity is approached. Then, allow each participant to talk a little bit about their own personal experience.

I acknowledge that not everyone is going to agree with me, nor will everyone find my theories or methods to their liking. I said it before, I'll state it again: if there was one way to go about having a conversation about race and identity, we'd all be doing it that way.

However, there isn't one way to have this discussion, so I, along with many other people trying to do this work, am offering a variety of different methods, styles, theories, and ways in which we can attempt to bridge this divide. It's not math or science, there isn't one proven or set formula that works for everyone in every situation. Acknowledge that, then try something: be open. Listen, and don't judge.

But the hushing of the criticism of honest opponents is a dangerous thing. It leads some of the best of the critics to unfortunate silence and paralysis of effort, and others to burst into speech so passionately and intemperately as to lose listeners.

W. E. B. DU BOIS
THE SOULS OF BLACK FOLKS

TOOL

Recognize there isn't any one way to have a conversation about identity and race. We all have different experiences and therefore bring different points of view to the table—this is actually the strength of our collective spirit, our diversity.

ACTION

Share your experience with coming to understand your race/identity (at this stage/time in your life).

STARTING POINTS

Establish a nonthreatening environment where what is said there, stays there. (I would say "safe," but many people have co-opted the word as being a place for snowflakes!)

Respect people's confidentiality.

In a small group of people I suggest sharing about the following:

- What is your earliest race-related memory?
- What age were you?
- What emotions were attached?
- Did you tell someone how you felt?
- How did you make sense of it?
- Do you have any memory of when you first realized you were _____?

Go around the group, each taking a turn to share without interruption from anyone.

FOUR

We Can Disagree so Long as We're Not Disagreeable

Throughout Obama's first term, Tea Party activists voiced their complaints in racist terms. Activists brandished signs warning that Obama would implement "white slavery," waved the Confederate flag, depicted Obama as a witch doctor, and issued calls for him to "go back to Kenya." Tea Party supporters wrote "satirical" letters in the name of "We Colored People" and stoked the flames of birtherism. One of the Tea Party's most prominent sympathizers, the radio host Laura Ingraham, wrote a racist tract depicting Michelle Obama gorging herself on ribs, while Glenn Beck said the president was a "racist" with a "deep-seated hatred for white people."

TA-NEHISI COATES
WE WERE EIGHT YEARS IN POWER

During a workshop following a performance for the senior class of one of the top boarding schools in the country, I ran into some disagreeable resistance. I usually open a session by offering to answer any questions students might have had regarding the issues my show exposes, before I get into the substance of the workshop. A stocky White boy with a bit of an aggressive approach wanted to know how I felt about a recent series of protests regarding inappropriate costumes being worn to campus parties: "Can you comment on the stupid situation regarding Halloween costumes at Yale?" I surmised from the way he spoke and how he'd framed the question that he was looking for a confrontation. His question referred to an incident that took place at Yale prior to campus Halloween celebrations in 2015. The Intercultural Affairs Committee had sent out an email asking students to be culturally sensitive when selecting outfits to wear, urging them to steer clear of costumes that could offend minority students. A faculty member who was also an administrator at a student residence, offended by what she perceived as an affront to free speech, pushed back with a passive-aggressive reply suggesting students should be free to express themselves in whatever way they see fit, no matter if it offends. Of course, all hell broke lose on Yale's campus, with students protesting and demanding what they saw as their First Amendment rights being trampled upon. This all seems quaint in the shadow of more recent revelations about blackface (as well as inappropriate KKK costumes and racial slurs) among several elected officials in Virginia during their college days some twenty years ago. However, at this boarding school not far from New Haven, this student was questioning what he saw as an absurd policy of appeasement and a crushing sense of being told what he could and could not say. "Why all the fuss about language and outfits that are offensive? Why can't people just get over it? We all get offended at times by what people say, so what?!"

"You are certainly correct. We have all experienced some form of offense during our lives," I told him. "There is not one person in this room who has not been hurt by something someone has said.

Words are like weapons and often they do serious injury. However," I added, "with freedoms come responsibilities, and I feel we need to step up and accept those responsibilities."

"I have the right to offend," he replied.

"Look," I countered, "I would never suggest censorship as a means to control what you see as your right, but is it really our job, our responsibility to offend? What may seem fun or appropriate for the offender may not be so for those offended."

I sensed he wasn't happy with my answer, feeling strongly about his rights being violated. He cared little for how his right to offensive speech might affect others. But our exchange seemed to stir things up, and hands shot up all across the room of approximately 115 students—a room, I should mention, with a total of five visible Black students, three possibly Hispanic, and at least half a dozen Asian. Another White boy was interested in how I now identified with my new racial background, a question I am frequently asked.

"Trying to explain one's identity," I started, "can often be much more complicated than the simple methods we have provided people with." I then gave a description of the US Census form and the confusion it can engender, reading as an example a portion of the 2010 form:

8. Is Person 1 of Hispanic, Latino, or Spanish origin?
☐ No, not of Hispanic, Latino, or Spanish origin
☐ Yes, Mexican, Mexican Am., Chicano
☐ Yes, Puerto Rican
☐ Yes, Cuban
☐ Yes, another Hispanic, Latino, or Spanish origin—Print origin, for example, Argentinean, Colombian, Dominican, Nicaraguan, Salvadoran, Spaniard, and so on.

9. What is Person 1's race? Mark X in one or
more boxes.

☐ White

☐ Black, African Am., or Negro

☐ American Indian or Alaska Native

☐ Asian Indian

☐ Chinese

☐ Filipino

☐ Japanese

☐ Korean

☐ Vietnamese

☐ Native Hawaiian

☐ Guamanian or Chamorro

☐ Samoan

☐ Other Pacific Islander—Print race, for example,
Fijian, Tongan, and so on.

☐ Other Asian—Print race, for example, Hmong,
Laotian, Thai, Pakistani, Cambodian, and so on.

☐ Some other race—Print race.

"Looking at question 9, I simply want to ask, why is White the first box?" A few students looked around, dumbfounded by what seemed, by the looks on their faces, to be a stupid question. I quickly followed half-jokingly with, "Look, I'm just asking for two reasons. First, if we generally list things in some kind of alphabetical order, last I checked White starts with a W and that would dictate a different order in this list. We all realize why it's the first box . . . it is the predominant race in this country. For those who consider themselves White, how would it make you feel if it wasn't the first box? Would you feel less powerful? Less dominant? Less in control? Second, I am sure many people checked the White box—millions and millions in fact—and might not even have given it a second thought. However, there are many White people who do not see themselves as White . . . they see themselves as Italian-American, or Irish-American, or Swedish-American, so the White box doesn't seem fair to them."

I then addressed the next box: Black, African American, or Negro. "And when did the term *Negro* make it back into our lexicon? That's a term used during the late fifties, early sixties. Who brought this back, and what made them think people of color still identified in this way?" I continued by asking about the now long list of racial categories and wondering when did all of these become part of what we consider the conversation about—or rather, definition of—race?

Finally, I challenged them to explain the difference between "origin," used to describe Hispanic people in question 8, and "race," used to describe a growing list of people in question 9. What is the difference between origin and race? There is no correct or agreed-upon answer to this question, as the confusion about the US Census form happens practically every ten years.[7]

"In choosing my own identity I often tell people that I see myself as I talk about at the end of my play, AAA or African American Armenian, but even that is a simplistic way to describe oneself. The way we see ourselves is quite often not the way others see us."

The same student who asked me about my identity then stated that he didn't really care about how people saw him and thus the identity question was silly in his eyes.

"Really? You don't care how other people may misperceive

---

[7] Visit the US Census website, https://www.census.gov/history/www/through_the_decades/questionnaires/1890_2.html, to see how the forms have evolved over decades and how the racial check boxes have changed.

who you truly are? What if there are stereotypes that happened to be attached to that misperception?"

"What do you mean?" he asked me.

"For instance, you are a tall, blond-haired, White teenager dressed in a polo shirt, Dockers pants, and docksider shoes who attends an elite, mostly White, private boarding school in the East. These descriptors carry stereotypes which are used by people to assess you personally. You're okay with someone thinking you are a stubborn, naive, insensitive, White teen?"

"No."

I then suggested that that might be how people see him, and although he may not think he is affected by it, does that still make it right that we use that system to judge people?

"Yeah, I guess so. So what?"

"I find it hard to believe that if you found yourself in a position in which you were applying for something, let's say a job or a scholarship, and someone judged you negatively simply by your appearance without having had any conversation with you, that you'd be okay with that!"

He waved me off abruptly, shook his head, and smirked as if my comments were ridiculous. "I could care less," he answered indignantly, yet clearly frustrated by my pushback. He was a part of the dominant or default race—White—and therefore seemed to have little attachment to specific race or culture markers (the result of White privilege). The hand of a young African American girl shot up instantly, and I called on her.

"What do you think about reverse racism?" she asked me directly, then she slowly surveyed the room as if checking to see how her White classmates would respond. I noticed that, back in the corner of the room, the young White man who had strongly advocated for his right to offend was smiling as he leaned forward, awaiting my reply.

"What do you mean 'reverse racism'?" I asked.

"You know . . . do you think it exists?"

"There is no reverse racism," I stated matter-of-factly, "not in this country anyway. There is prejudice, but racism is defined as a system of discrimination and oppression based on the belief that one race is superior to another. Prejudice, on the other hand, is usually negative feelings or treatment toward a thing or group of people. To say there is reverse racism, reverse oppression, is ridiculous. There is no Black KKK. There was never a poll tax on White voters. Black people had to endure separate drinking fountains and were forced into seats at the back of buses. White people weren't subjected to a system of sterilization when deemed by society to be unfit for parenthood, or a well-recorded track record of discrimination in housing, mortgage lending rates, or even school disciplinary actions."

The young woman seemed quite satisfied and relieved with my response as she took note of the room. I, on the other hand, sensed a general uneasiness in the room. The young White man in the corner who had argued for his right to offend was quietly but animatedly taking offense by shaking his head and waving off my response with his circle of friends. Others shook their heads in disbelief as they quietly whispered to their seatmates about what seemed to be their dissatisfaction with my reply. I could have continued and given those with potential counter arguments an opportunity to respond, but I felt the need to push on with the actual workshop. I wanted to turn the energy around and lighten the mood, fearing things could get out of hand. This probably could have been an opportunity to try to facilitate a much larger dialogue, but with over a hundred people in the room, I knew the chances of it veering out of control were strong.

So I jumped in, changing the subject slightly, and began to lead the group through activities that provide an engaging way to take a look at the stereotypes we all have. I ran through a couple of fun exercises to get them to confront their own biases and discomfort. There was another exercise I was hoping to get to, but my time was up. It had been a challenging session, and I was relieved to be able to let them go. As is often the case, several students approached me before they headed to the exits. One in particular was the White boy who had claimed he did not care about what people thought about him.

He started with, "So you really don't feel like there is any reverse racism in the US?"

"Based on the definitions I explained, no. Prejudice, yes. Reverse racism, no."

"Then how do you feel about affirmative action?" he asked with a slight grin, hoping he had laid a trap into which I would fall freely.

"How do I feel about it? Well, unfortunately, I feel some form of it is necessary to help create balance in a system that is still quite unequal."

"So you believe that preferences should be given to those who may not have the same level of knowledge or achievement than others?"

"Some students of color are not offered the same advantages, or for that matter are not even on the same playing field. When we have a majority of students of color who once again find themselves at a disadvantage because they go to primarily all-minority schools, which have significantly less educational resources than other, all-White schools, then yes, we need to create some type of balance."

"But what about the disadvantage or discrimination that creates for those who have worked especially hard to get to where they are."

"I am not suggesting the current system makes complete sense, and you may see this as discrimination or reverse racism, but there's no comparison. Students of color are at such a disadvantage when it comes to the overall educational opportunities they are offered, and there needs to be some way to help create better balance. And, of course, there are what are known as legacy admissions—a leg up for those whose family members have attended a certain school. A vast majority of legacy admissions are for White students. That cycle perpetuates itself over and over again, leaving those without a connection to a particular history at a particular educational institution at a disadvantage."

What I wanted to say was, *Did you look around the room at your senior class and notice there were only five Black students out of 115 in the room? And you're worried about the college you are going to get into and whether or not a Black student is going to take your "entitled" slot? Why do you think there are so few Black students at your school and does that somehow seem fair to you? Do you think you've all started out on equal footing?*

But I did not.

He wasn't entirely satisfied by my pointing out the specific disadvantage for Black students of legacy admissions, but I felt this had certainly made him think more deeply about how he sees what he perceives to be reverse racism via affirmative action. At least this exchange had a sense of civility to it, as opposed to the prior exchange with the student who felt he had the right to be offensive and to offend.

* * * *

If we really want to get to what has now become the root of our collective disagreeableness, then an obvious place to start is in our politics . . . especially in our current state. There have always been actors on the political stage who have used race, racism, dog whistles, and other inflammatory language to divide Americans. Dog whistles—coded political language—might be described as derogatory expressions that speak to a subset of a certain group of American voters. Just as a real dog whistle is so quiet that only a dog can hear it, these expressions speak to those people more attuned to responding to language that might seem racially inflammatory. However, even in difficult times, political leaders, presidents especially, have sought to find ways to bring people together in a united cause. This is unfortunately not the case with our current administration. Vilification of different types of people has never resulted in bringing us together. Blaming others for our problems just passes the blame rather than accepting responsibility. As Americans we have become the champions of blame. I've got nothing against lawyers, but no other nation is as lawyered up as we are, ready to sue at a moment's notice.

Although some politicians use coded language, others aren't nearly as subtle. Steve King, a Republican congressman from Iowa, just comes right out and states his racist beliefs, albeit he *seems* to be oblivious of their actual meaning or impact. I've read that some Iowans don't think he actually means everything he says, yet why would they tolerate such ugly, divisive, racist rhetoric? Shouldn't we hold all Americans to some standard of decency and tolerance? Louie Gohmert, a Republican congressman from Texas, speaks in similar ways, as did Michele Bachmann, a former Republican congresswoman (and presidential candidate) from Minnesota. Tom Tancredo, a former Republican congressman from Colorado (as well as serving as Mitt Romney's campaign operative) is another who just speaks his mind with little filtering or any use for a dog-whistle shield.[8]

---

8 Steve King, who famously described Mexican immigrants as having "calves the size of cantaloupes" from hauling drugs across the border, has sided and supported White nationalists and sports a Confederate flag on his desk (interview on NewsMax, July 2013). Louie Gohmert, one of the original birthers, claimed that hate crime legislation would lead to necrophilia (from Gohmert's website April, 27, 2009). Michele Bachmann frequently claimed she acted

Then there are the up-and-coming, fully out of the closet, racist White nationalist candidates who recently ran for seats in Republican primaries across the country (perhaps not what the Republican Party had hoped for): Patrick Little in California (avowed neo-Nazi ran unsuccessfully for California State Senate in April 2018, capturing 1.2 percent of the vote), Arthur Jones in Illinois (a Holocaust denier who ran for US Congress unsuccessfully in November 2018, capturing 25 percent of the vote), Russell Walker in North Carolina (an avowed White supremacist, lost a 2018 race for the state House but captured 37 percent of the vote), Paul Nehlen in Wisconsin (the White nationalist who enjoyed the support of Sarah Palin, Ann Coulter, and Steve Bannon but lost his House race for Paul Ryan's congressional seat in 2016), and Corey Stewart in Virginia (a pro-Confederate conservationist who lost his US Senate race to Tim Kaine in 2018) all espouse or have supported hate speech from a nationalistic or neo-Nazi angle. This in-your-face, out-in-the-open kind of racism, nationalism, and anti-Semitism has historically been more hushed, part of the fringe elements of society. Currently, it's up front and center. By the time this book is published we may have moved on from these names, but sadly there will undoubtedly be others to replace them.

Then there are those who tilt right in the media and often use racist, offensive, derogatory language when describing others: Sean Hannity, Ann Coulter, Rush Limbaugh, Alex Jones, Laura Ingraham, Pat Buchanan, Steve Bannon, and Milo Yiannopoulos are prominent examples. There are actually many more, but you

on direct orders from God himself and was staunchly antigay, declaring that same-sex marriage and Obama would be the cause of the Rapture (on radio show host Jan Markell's broadcast in March 2015). Tom Tancredo called for the end of illegal and legal immigration, is in favor of bringing back a literacy test for our electoral process, and proposed dropping a bomb on Mecca should there be another terrorist attack on our country (on YouTube, August 2007).

get the idea; there are many people trafficking in terribly offensive, sometimes hate-filled, language. How exactly does this serve us? What kind of unity or progress does this provide?

I would be remiss if I didn't address another political actor in our nation's racial dynamic. I hesitate to even mention his name, as doing so gives him power (of acknowledgment), but the depths to which this person sinks are truly astounding, and those who follow his work (who most likely would never pick up this book) are cult-like conspiracy theorists (and I am afraid there may be many!). I am speaking of Dinesh D'Souza, the recently pardoned right-wing conspiracy theorist and provocateur. He calls himself a conservative thinker, author, and filmmaker. It's difficult to write calmly about a man who promotes himself shamelessly, who peddles alternative history and indulges in race-baiting, sowing division with his aggrandizing. A brown man of Indian descent, he has often played his own race card as if his brownness qualifies as American Blackness.

D'Souza, as a college student and writer for the conservative *Dartmouth Review*, oversaw an article that outed liberal homosexuals on campus and edited a "jive column," a takedown of college affirmative action written in Ebonics. In his 1995 book titled *The End of Racism* he defended Jim Crow. In 2007 he claimed the left was responsible for 9/11. His claim to fame was probably the 2012 documentary titled *2016: Obama's America* in which he claimed the president was a Manchurian candidate, a plant who was brainwashed by his Kenyan father to destroy the US government from within. In his next film, in 2014, he claimed slavery wasn't all that bad. Why have there been so many White people making this claim, from Bill O'Reilly, formerly at FOX, to the former White House chief of staff John Kelly, to members of the organization Sons of Confederate Veterans?

This is where we're at: we're now arguing about facts. What was once considered factual is now considered fake. Even the words *racism* and *racist* have changed in meaning. As the word is currently interpreted, in order to be considered a racist, you have to have lynched someone; and since there hasn't been a lynching in a long time, there must not be any more racists. Right?

Who are the real racists? Who are the real fascists?

What is considered to be the last known lynching in America took place in Alabama in 1981. White supremacy was the motto of the Alabama Democratic Party until 1966, and Mississippi did not ratify the Thirteenth Amendment outlawing slavery until 1995. More recently, in 2015, nine Black people were murdered in a church in Charleston, and quite anonymously during that same year twenty transgender people were also murdered. The year 2016 saw the election of Donald Trump; the immediate rise of violence at his campaign rallies, provoked by his prompting, was then translated into a considerable rise in all forms of racist language, acts, and taunts across America. In 2017 during the White nationalist rally and subsequent riots in Charlottesville, a female antiracist protester was run over and killed, an event which the president described as "good people on both sides." That year also recorded an enormous spike in anti-Semitic threats. In 2018 these threats mutated into the death of eleven at a synagogue in Pittsburgh. These hateful acts were all occurring in the shadow of a Muslim ban, prompting an 83 percent increase in anti-Muslim threats.

Why are we so disagreeable toward one another? Can we all agree that hate is a poison?

* * * *

I gave a speech at an educational conference once and began by asking for all the realists in the room to raise their hands . . . a good number of hands went up and some laughs followed. I then asked for all the capitalists in the room to raise their hands and practically the entire room raised their hands. Folks laughed as they looked around to see who raised their hand, and maybe more importantly who didn't. I followed this by asking to see the hands of activists, humanists, idealists, feminists, and finally ending by asking for the hands of all the racists. No hands went up for racists. No one wants to identify as racist. Members of the KKK won't identify as racist. Even racists don't want to identify as being racist.

These days, being disagreeable seems to be a badge of honor. Everywhere you look there is yet another story about someone talking back, talking smack, putting down, or what some of these disagreeable folks might see as standing up for what they believe. You read about this all the time, and as if it is not enough to simply read an article about people's disagreeable nature, you are then subjected to disagreeable comments following that article. We've all seen the comment sections attached to stories at various news (and social media) sites. Anyone who has read them can attest to the general offensive nature of many commenters.

I first became hyperaware of the offensive nature of these comment sections when I began doing interviews with various news organizations regarding my story and upon the publication of my memoir. Visiting the websites of the news organizations that featured articles written about my story, I often found several readers who had posted uninformed, and sometimes nasty, comments (some quite personal). Thankfully, comments that bordered on offensive were quickly removed by the news outlet's internal review board, but obviously some folks just couldn't hold back their thoughts! People called me all kinds of derogatory names without even having met me! At first I was shocked at the level of hatred and racism directed toward me by those who had simply read a story about me searching for my biological father and discovering he was Black. It also shocked me to discover that sometimes even readers who identified as Black were offended by my embrace of a new family and identity. Some were affronted by my White privilege, as if I had some kind of choice in my skin tone. One Black reader was insulted I chose to "pass" for White, yet clearly for most of my life I didn't even know I was half Black and therefore was not consciously passing.[9] Although a majority of the comments were for the most part positive or complimentary, after a while I realized I should probably stop reading these comment sections. I found them personally debilitating and difficult to erase from memory.

Social media—Twitter and Facebook among others—is another area where people have let loose with their racism and offensive comments. As a part of my work to try to forge what I had hope will be a national dialogue, I created a Facebook page and a Twitter profile to share articles and pieces that dealt with identity issues and to promote my tour schedule. I quickly learned this was another area where I was vulnerable to attack by people who disagreed with me and were sometimes disagreeable. Anonymous people also post disagreeable messages on updates at the Incognito Facebook page. Even something as innocuous as a tour date could sometimes be subject to a snide, snarky, or offensive retort.

Twitter was equally as unnerving since people can troll with obnoxious comments and ridiculous ripostes. My own personal way of dealing with these was to ignore them, but that didn't stop people from posting offensive replies. As things led up to the 2016 election and the online chatter and postings became more and more divisive and offensive, I began to realize the folly in trying to forge a dialogue online. I subsequently deleted my Facebook

---

[9] Passing is a huge and sensitive issue in the Black community. For more on that, see Brando Skyhorse and Lisa Page, eds., *We Wear the Mask: Fifteen True Stories of Passing in America* (Boston: Beacon, 2017).

and Twitter accounts following the election of 2016, preferring to foster constructive dialogue face to face. If my goal was to create a space where we could talk about extremely sensitive and divisive issues of great importance, social media could not substitute for real authentic dialogue. Dialogue happens in person. There are some who believe they are participating in what is considered dialogue online. I do not believe this to be true dialogue, at least certainly not dialogue that can bolster any true sense of understanding. Part of the problem is that writing has limitations in that each reader interprets what they read in their own unique way. This is sometimes exacerbated by our differing definitions of words, whether from different intellectual or different cultural backgrounds.

Add to this the anonymity of online participants in social media, the fact that we cannot entirely know or understand others' backgrounds. What happens quite often is that we end up reading posts from people online whom we know very little about. We might start on a friend's page, reading a post they've made about, let's say, Black Lives Matter. We follow our friend's initial post by reading all the subsequent posts by friends and friends of friends, and so on. Some responses we may agree with, others we don't or may find offensive. We add our two cents to the feed and maybe click on a link that someone (assumed to be a friend of our friend) has posted. Some of these people and posts have been revealed to be from entities who are not actually people. They are from bots . . . automatic posting systems design to sow discord (some controlled by Russian operatives, we are told). But the point is that many of these posts are from people we know absolutely nothing about. Is this any way to have a dialogue about issues that can be quite complicated and divisive? Excuse the pun, but this feels like a black and white conversation which avoids, or rather has little interest in, the nuances of color.

This is not to suggest that all posts and posters on these platforms are guilty of sharing offensive, racist, or inflammatory thoughts and beliefs. There are certainly many decent people connecting, sharing stories and photos about their lives and their families. Not everyone with a Facebook page is caught up in the day-to-day blah, blah, blah on social (or perhaps even conventional) media. However, every one of us is affected by both the explicit and implicit biases we carry. Those are facts we cannot ignore, something worth exposing in hopes of change.

There is so much anger, so much vehemence and vitriol online these days. A study done by Chinese researchers discovered that anger spreads faster online and is more prevalent than sadness, disgust, or even joy.[10] Weren't we told that venting could be therapeutic as far back as Freud in 1885? As unreal as we may think the online world is, those of us who visit there often are taking in, and taking on, the anger we see there. Science has proven this anger spreads and grows more quickly than positive emotions. If they are right, where does this anger go?

The anger is everywhere, the media tells us. It is what contributed to the election of an offensive person as president. Some simply see him as speaking his mind. Would those who think he is merely speaking his mind—when he describes people as rapists (who aren't) or slimeballs (certainly not the worst thing he's called someone), or refers to shithole countries (derogatory language)—feel comfortable letting their kids talk this way? This is not a book about politics, and it is probably pretty

---

[10] In a 2013 study of over 200,000 internet users done by Beijhang University, researchers found that anger spread faster than sadness or joy among the 70 million messages they collected; R. Fan, J. Zhao, Y. Chen, and K. Xu, "Anger Is More Influential than Joy: Sentiment Correlation in Weibo," *PLoS ONE* 9, no. 10 (October 15, 2014): e110184a. A follow-up study by researchers at the Wharton School reached the same conclusions; Jeremy A. Yip and Maurice E. Schweitzer, "Mad and Misleading: Incidental Anger Promotes Deception," *Organizational Behavior and Human Decision Processes* 137 (November 2016): 207–17.

obvious where I fall on the ideological spectrum, but I do think it is still important for us to have reasoned debate. I acknowledge that there are many people who see the world differently, and I may not always agree with their views nor they with mine. But I do not think it is helping any of us find our commonalities by being disagreeable. This kind of tactic, or whatever you want to call it, is simply pushing us away from those common bonds, and away from becoming more successful at being us (both the collective us, as in neighbors, colleagues, and friends, and as in the political and ideological United States).

We cherish our right to free speech; it is an essential part of who we are as Americans. There are many other places in the world where that right does not exist, and some are becoming less and less free. However, with freedoms come responsibilities. Not many of us think about the responsibility of free speech. We are free to say whatever we like and quick to defend that right. We all must recognize that there are consequences to our actions and words. Likewise, if we truly allow freedom to worship any God of our choosing, then we can't go around blowing up the mosques or churches of those we may not understand and expect not to bear the consequences of those actions. If we engender the right of a free and open press, then we must also understand that censoring them would have a devastating consequence. Much like freedom of the press, we must also understand that freedom of speech carries consequences.

Every person in society has at some time in their life been hurt by something someone has said. For some that hurt never goes away; for others it may take years to subside, and yet for others it may be just a fleeting moment before we strike back. Words can be used like weapons. However many of us are often oblivious to the power our words have and perhaps never take responsibility for the damage they cause.

As an example, I am often asked about the use of the N-word. It is pretty much widely accepted that this word is off limits to

White people. However, there are many in the Black community who also are deeply troubled by its use in their communities. Now that I am half Black, where does that put me? I didn't grow up using it, was not raised in a Black household or community, and to most people I project as a White male. Yet I am biracial, mixed, half Black. Where do I stand when it comes to the rule about N-word usage? Is there a guidebook for lighter-skinned Blacks? Can I use it, would that be proper? Black rap artists fling it like candy, which has led to White rap fans repeating what they hear, shocking those witnessing their mimicry. More importantly, why would I want to use the word? It's a linguistic gun that hurts indiscriminately.

I am not suggesting censorship of the N-word. As an artist and creator I believe in the importance of free expression . . . sometimes to the point of making the audience uncomfortable (as some feel during my play). But I would never suggest, as did the New York City Council, in a mostly symbolic gesture in late April 2007, that banning the use of the N-word would make people feel better.

What if we took responsibility for use of our words? If you feel you really need to use certain words, consider first who will be the recipient of that language and how it might affect them. If you have doubts as to how it may be received, then maybe you might consider a different set of words, perhaps less inflammatory or divisive. Is it so much to ask of ourselves to try and be more civil? In an age when our president throws caution to the wind by using derogatory and incendiary language, tacitly suggesting others have the same permission to do likewise, civility could help immensely. If we expect to restore what's United about our States, then taking responsibility for our words and actions while treating others with respect should be mandatory.

It is entirely up to the American people and our representatives whether or not they are going to face and deal with and embrace this stranger who they have maligned so long. What white people have to do is try and find out in their own hearts why it was necessary to have a "nigger" in the first place, because I'm not a nigger, I'm a man. But if you think I'm a nigger, it means you need him. . . . If I'm not the nigger here and you invented him, you the white people invented him, then you've got to find out why. And the future of the country depends on that, whether or not it is able to ask that question.

JAMES BALDWIN
THE NEGRO AND THE AMERICAN PROMISE

TOOL

We can disagree so long as we're not disagreeable. Take responsibility for the language we use—freedom of speech carries responsibilities.

ACTION

In conversation, remain civil no matter the topic! Don't let disagreement or anger control you.

STARTING POINTS

- Don't avoid political or hot-button issues, but rather try approaching them from purely a personal perspective.
- Don't avoid discussing the day's news—we all hear and read it. By avoiding it, it becomes the elephant in the room. Remember to use civility as a guide.
- Listen respectfully without interrupting and when sharing, don't monopolize the conversation.
- Silence gives consent. When you hear or see something that is offensive, racist, homophobic, or derogatory about a marginalized group, speak up... and do so in a respectful manner.

FIVE

Get Comfortable Being Uncomfortable

Not everything that is faced can be changed;
But nothing can be changed until it is faced.

JAMES BALDWIN

I AM NOT YOUR NEGRO

Following a show at a college in Bellingham, Washington, a young White student proceeded to ask a question about how I now perceived myself with my newfound racial identity. But in asking, he struggled to find a term for "racial identity" that he felt comfortable with. He tripped all over his words as he carefully, cautiously searched to find a word that might seem less offensive, or perhaps less likely to be mistaken as racist, in describing my Black identity. He tried out "urban," then corrected himself with "African American," and finally pivoted to "racial identity," unsure which term was proper or less offensive. He was sincerely trying to get it right, but what term is the correct one to use? Why is identity, specifically a Black identity, so often difficult for White people to talk about? And sometimes even for Black people? Do White people struggle with identifying themselves as being White? My story certainly provoked, in him and for others in the room that day, the question of what does it mean to be Black. The corollary, quite obviously, is what does it mean to be White? Are we willing to go there and talk about these things? If we struggle—as this young man did—just to find a term that seems comfortable or appropriate, how do we expect to even have this conversation?

Talking about race and identity is uncomfortable. People of all races, genders, sexual orientations, and a slew of other identity markers all struggle at times to engage comfortably in these conversations in mixed company. As I pointed out earlier, even those of us working in the field of diversity and inclusion can run into walls occasionally. More and more educational institutions and corporations employ multicultural directors or diversity officers to facilitate both nurturing diverse talent and creating an inclusive environment within which to study or work. These positions, mostly held by people of color or women, are fraught with challenges. Depending upon the commitment of those in charge of the educational institutions or corporations, funding can be scarce, hindering efforts. Often there is disinterest on the part of those who feel diversity and inclusion should have to include them (i.e., White people). Efforts to get people to buy into and comprehend the importance and value of diversity and inclusion are rebuffed and ignored. There are numerous studies that show how greater diversity and better inclusion can improve outcomes, results, and bottom lines. Studies by McKinsey, Katherine W. Phillips, Josh Bersin, and Sylvia Ann Hewlett, Melinda Marshall, and Laura Sherbin, to name just a few, are conclusive evidence of increased outcomes.[11] Why more

---

[11] Vivian Hunt, Dennis Layton, and Sara Prince, *Diversity Matters* (McKinsey and Co., February 2, 2015); Katherine W. Phillips, "How Diversity Makes Us Smarter," *Scientific American*, October 1, 2014; Josh Bersin, "Why Diversity and Inclusion Has Become a Business Priority," December 7, 2015, https://joshbersin. com/2015/12/why-diversity-and-inclusion-will-be-a-top-priority-for-2016/; and Sylvia Ann Hewlett, Melinda Marshall, and Laura Sherbin, "How Diversity Can Drive Innovation," *Harvard Business Review*, December 2013.

companies don't take advantage is a complicated maze of mirrortocracy (hiring those who look like those doing the hiring), entrenched White as the default, resistance to change, institutional racism, and the ever-repeated refrain, "Can't find qualified applicants," which has resulted in the sharp growth of the diversity and inclusion field.

* * * *

Numerous times I've spoken to multicultural directors at very tony (and primarily White) private high schools about the need for programming at their institutions. They become excited about my presentation and what they see as the very real need for it at their schools. We've even booked dates, and sometimes issued contracts for a particular date, time, and place. Then, as has been the case at too many schools to remember, they disappear. Some don't return calls and emails; others say the date chosen is unsustainable or their funds are exhausted. Several times I've spoken to multicultural directors who tell me they couldn't get buy-in from their administration, fearing, they were told, that the students weren't ready for this type of dialogue. (If that's the case, why have a position of multicultural director?) At one extremely wealthy school in a very affluent White area of Florida, the multicultural director, an African American woman, broke down in tears on the phone, sharing with me her frustrations and anger about the lack of support for her work. She expressed her embarrassment regarding our many-months-long correspondence leading up to a confirmed presentation date and issuance of a contract that now would not be signed. Sadly, later that year she wrote to inform me she was leaving the school (and the state).

* * * *

Having traveled around the country for so many years, I have gotten to know a good number of administrators who've become supporters of my work. Over the years some of these have transferred to different schools around the country, and they reach out to bring my work to their new educational institutions. Thus I found myself preparing for a visit to a school in Maine, where the new head was someone who'd followed my work when he was previously employed at a school near Philadelphia. A couple weeks before the show I got a call from the head of the school, who'd suddenly encountered a great deal of pushback from teachers worried about how my presentation might disrupt the delicate racial balance with their burgeoning African immigrant community. They feared my story would open doors to a conversation on race they were unprepared to have.

This is a common fear I hear from many educators—mostly White, but also some of color (because they tend to be the only faculty member of color on their campus and are thus viewed as the "expert" on race—much like the sole student of color in a class is assumed to have all the answers to the questions on race). It's as if they are trying to avoid the conversation and thus avoid the uncomfortableness they'd rather not be a part of. Teachers also often feel that, because they are the teacher, they must be the expert in the classroom at all times, that they must have answers to all the questions their students might put forth.

In Maine, the head of the school, probably because we had known each other for years, was now asking if I could come to their school a day earlier than originally planned to meet with teachers and hopefully diminish their fears. He was essentially asking me to give the teachers tools to help them cope.

So I arrived a day earlier, and during the afternoon, when class was over, I met with a group of about a dozen teachers who peppered me with questions and expressed their fears. A few were concerned that, by presenting the show, they were opening themselves to charges of racism. They feared the show would discuss issues of racism which their students had no context to understand. They worried in particular about the response from their students who had recently immigrated from Africa, and they wanted to know how did I (and the administration) expect them to tackle that. The conversation with teachers grew testy at times, as the onslaught was nonstop, filled with trepidation and incredulousness.

I was shocked at how thoroughly these educators had misinterpreted my work and story and let their fears run wild. The play isn't really about racism or prejudice, I told them, but rather about a personal journey that unfolds like a mystery. There are certainly a set of stereotypes I put forth (on purpose mind you!), and these allow for an opportunity to talk about how we all have some stereotypes that apply to us. The stereotypes are a means— or theatrical device if you will—to talk about how we judge one another. I suggested to the teachers that they needed to get comfortable being uncomfortable and that in a classroom, especially, it is vitally important to be honest about that, to let your students know you don't have all the answers. Let them know this is a personal story, then get comfortable asking them about theirs. Let them know there isn't a set formula to having these conversations . . . and that's okay.

By the end of the tough, combative session, some seemed to be a little more at ease. There was still tension from not knowing what to expect (or how to deal with it), but I sensed an overall exhale from the room as I left for dinner that evening. There had been one woman in particular, an older White woman, a teacher for many years at the school, who'd been especially anxious about my program. I could tell she was not totally convinced her fears weren't warranted, but she did reluctantly thank me upon leaving the room.

The next morning, the show was received very well by the students and staff. They were an extremely respectful crowd, responding vocally without fear of being judged. I was met with a standing ovation, which, following the previous day's session with teachers, felt like a vindication. The dialogue was rich with questions about identity and race with many students lining up at the microphones set in the aisles. We discussed the stereotypes, census forms, identity issues, and more. There were so many students looking to talk that we had to cut them off for lack of time.

I had agreed in advance to a meeting with a group of students who were part of the racial alliance on campus, and over lunch we continued a deeper dialogue about all the issues the play exposes. During the conversation a student asked how my wife had responded when she learned the news of my background. Usually the question I get quite frequently, when someone notices my wedding band, is "Did you marry the Brit?" referring to my British ex-girlfriend, Jo, who is mentioned in the play. I did not, I answer, which is then almost always followed by "Did you marry a Black woman?" I am amused by this line of questions, but it also makes a great deal of sense to me. They have just followed me on this remarkable journey during which the Brit is a major character. I never resolve her story line, so it naturally makes sense people would ask. Here, I mentioned this to the group off-handedly and then proceeded to answer the question, talking about my wife's Jewish heritage, for her background has further resonance in the dialogue about identity. What is a Jew? Is it a race or a religion? At least, that was how I remembered the conversation at lunch. A few weeks later, I received a call from one of the faculty members, warning me that the students would like to send me a letter in which they express some troubles they had with my lunch visit. I received the following letter from the students just days later:

Dear Mr. Fosberg,

Your one act play *Incognito* was captivating, and your thoughts about identity were presented in an entertaining voice. Issues of identity and race are not always talked about so freely at our school, and the play began a dialogue that is raising many important questions for the students and faculty.

As the members of the Racial Awareness group, we would like to share with you some of our observations about our meeting with you. In creating a community within our group, we abide by the important guidelines to listen carefully, ask questions openly and honestly, and validate all individual feelings. We assume good intentions of all participants who ask questions and offer ideas. When Christian asked you how your wife responded when she first learned of your background, you responded instead to a question you thought he might have asked—Is your wife white?—which you said would be racist. The fact that you responded to a question that he didn't ask made us wonder if you were really listening to us.

Labeling that question as racist made us all reluctant to talk further and share our ideas.

The members of [the racial alliance] welcome every opportunity provided to us to ask the hard questions about race, ethnicity, history, and culture. We thank you for encouraging our discussions through your presentation. We know we can learn so much from each other.

We wish you the best of luck on your journey and hope others will benefit from your story.

Obviously I must have been mistaken in how I remembered the conversation. I thought deeply about the lunch, our conversation, and how I remember people leaving the room that day. I decided I would write them an apology, with an explanation.

Thank you so much for your letter, response, and feedback regarding my recent visit to your campus. I am also quite pleased you took the time and energy to reach out and engage. The only way for us to move forward in opening up real change is to continue to forge ahead with constructive dialogue. I felt the need to respond in an effort to sustain that, and hope you will continue to engage in meaningful conversations about these tough issues.

As to your observation, I regret I have no recollection of saying what you heard me say. Although it appears I did not answer the specific question posed by Christian, I may have transposed the question since the answer to the one posed is boring to say the least. My wife had knowledge of my story/discovery before we met for the first time. She was aware of my background and the work I have been engaged in. Her response upon meeting was about what an amazing story I had. I have however quite often been asked the question of my wife's ethnicity. Since marrying last June and revealing this to audiences, people are curious as to whether she is black or white. I have never considered this question racist as indeed it is not, in my opinion. It shouldn't matter what race my wife is, but once I've revealed my newly discovered biraciality, people want to know. However, the question of her race and the answer I most often give expose how difficult it is to have this dialogue, as you so clearly point out in the beginning of your letter. My answer to the question I thought I was asked has always been that my wife is Jewish. I use this answer as a way to raise another very important issue about race, ethnicity and identity. Many people of the Jewish faith see themselves as Jews first. This "classification" provokes the question: What exactly is a Jew? A religion, an ethnicity, or a culture? Thus when answering the question of my wife's background, I always answer by saying she is Jewish in order to bring up another important conversation about identity. I do not recall saying the question was racist. And I do not remember at anytime during our lunch together any uncomfortableness or inhibitions in having an open dialogue. As a matter of fact, I recall many of you thanked me as you rushed off to your next class. I apologize for any misunderstanding, it was never my intention to invalidate or disrespect anyone's feelings.

This misunderstanding is, however, a perfect example of what prohibits us from having and sustaining important conversations about race. It is what I have tried to illustrate when talking about how in mixed company whites tend to approach the dialogue from a place of caution (some more than others) for fear of saying something wrong/racist/offensive, while people of color often seem ready to pounce on anyone or anything that sounds remotely racist, thus stifling whites' willingness to talk. We are polarized and thus, out of fear or inexperience by whites, and resentment or hurt by people of color, we tend to avoid open, honest dialogue.

If I said something that offended, or if someone provokes resentment or hurt with an offhand or even direct comment, we cannot allow that to stifle our efforts to converse. We must share our hurt, our pain, our opinions in an effort to better understand how we each feel about who we are. It is also important to remember that there is NOT ONE general experience; be you black, white, Asian, Hispanic, gay, straight, woman, whatever. There are many different experiences between people of the same categories, yet we tend to generalize, thus stereotyping a group. What may seem offensive to one black, white, woman, gay, older person, whomever . . . might not seem that way to another. However, if we allow something said to get in the way of further conversation, then we are perpetuating the status quo, which is to say, stifling further dialogue and stuck in the rut we find ourselves.

This important and HEALING dialogue is fraught with difficulties that are often beyond our comprehension. We recently experienced how difficult it is to engage in this conversation face to face—I seem to have said something that offended, causing you all (?) to be "reluctant to talk further and share" your ideas. Now we are writing to one another, *which is great*, but also fraught with misinterpretations of the written word. I have been railing about how destructive comment sections following online news articles can be. They do not allow us to SEE one another and put our whole being into perspective, our experiences, our facial expressions, our cultural perspectives, etc. Take a look at the comment section of any online news article that deals with issues of race. There have unfortunately been many of late, whether it is about the NBA Los Angeles Clippers' owner Donald Sterling, or the Nevada cattle rancher Cliven Bundy. You will be shocked by what you read and what seems to pass as "dialogue" in this country. I have had many articles written about me, and my work, and have gasped at some of the comments by people who know absolutely nothing about me. On top of that there is social media; Facebook and Twitter with 140 characters. Is this any way to have meaningful *dialogue*?

Finally, take a look at how race is covered by the media on television. In my experience, 9 times out of 10 when interviewed by a reporter it has been a person of color. Why does it seem only black reporters are asked to cover a dialogue about race? And what would it seem like to people of color if that reporter were white?

I could go on and on . . . and I am sorry it seems as though I inhibited your ability to do so with me on my visit. I hope this letter will provoke additional conversation, and I welcome an open line of communication in the future. Push on, ask questions, and don't allow your hurt or misunderstanding to get in the way of probing further. The only way we will have any kind of chance at making a real difference in the dialogue about race is to have more dialogue. Keep talking!

Sincerely,
Michael Fosberg

By the way, the teacher who had expressed such trepidation about my presentation and the problems the faculty might face in dealing with the aftermath wrote me a day later saying: "Michael, thank you for three things . . . the link to the portrait poems that will be used in advising, the candid conversation with us as faculty members, and for the wonderfully written and acted performance piece at assembly."

At a certain point I hope it will become vitally apparent to us that if we are to actually engage in meaningful conversations about race and identity, we must get comfortable being uncomfortable.

This acting axiom—one that many an acting teacher has expounded on—has proven to be a constant part of my experience as I travel across the country. In addition to the moments on stage when my show takes an unexpected turn due to something happening in the audience, or when I find myself in a tight spot during the talkback portion, I find myself shaken by the utter truth of this statement and attempt as best I can to embrace the unknown.

Getting comfortable being uncomfortable is not something most people feel any inclination to do. *Why would I want to do that?!* they cry. But the fact of the matter is most of us are uncomfortable at some point in our day. It may be just for a moment—spilling a cup of coffee or forgetting to make an important call—but there is most certainly a point in each day when we encounter an uncomfortable moment and we get through it. We can and must do the same with this vitally important conversation about race and identity.

* * * *

In February of 2016 I was asked to collaborate on a diversity training session at an oil refinery in the Midwest. An odd place, I thought to myself, and most likely one that would prove to be challenging. The daylong session was to open with my presentation, followed by a guided dialogue, then transition into an interactive portion led by diversity facilitators from the organization I was collaborating with. We had done a few of these very successful collaborations over the past few years and were excited to work together once again in such a challenging location. Using my presentation as a point of reference, they crafted a session that would dig deeper into the issues my life story exposed.

I knew little about oil refineries, but I imagined there were probably a good deal more production workers and operations people than executive and midlevel management. In other words, I expected a large number of attendees to be laborers on the front lines of the plant versus folks dressed in more formal business attire. Turned out I was right! The room soon filled with about thirty, more than half of them decked out in one-piece work coveralls stained with dirt and oil.

We were cramped in a tight, aging and battered, nondescript sort of classroom with participants seated at round tables. There was barely enough room for me to eek out space to perform, but I'd become accustomed to figuring out how to adapt my show for spaces of all kinds. I once did a presentation in a tiny *U*-shaped room filled with CDOs (chief diversity officers) of Fortune 500 companies, where I basically had to throw out all my blocking (the actor's movement on stage) and rework the show live on my feet in a space about six feet across and four feet deep, enough room for a speaker at a standard podium, but hardly enough for a play.

I figured the oil refinery would be a tough crowd—it was already a tough room—but nothing prepared me for what came next. The crowd was silent as they watched the play . . . no one seemed comfortable laughing out loud. I could, however, see people stifling their laughter! They were mostly attentive, and since I address the audience directly and can actually see everyone, their faces held most of the clues. The folks of color in the room would smile or grin during many moments during the show, but none felt comfortable enough to crack the silence of the room with an outright laugh. For the most part, the White people in the room remained silent as well; a few offered slight smiles, but in general, they didn't let their faces expose how they truly felt. I had a sense they were actively holding back, uncomfortably so.

When I asked for questions following the show, no one had any—which can sometimes be the case when nobody wants to be the first one out of the box—so I dove into my standard discussion about stereotypes. Who saw the Black characters as stereotypical? Who saw the White characters as stereotypes? This usually stimulates dialogue and further questions, however this time the room was silent.

A facilitator from the firm I was partnering with on this day-long program quickly piped in with a question about racial boxes and identity, which then led me into a discussion about the census. More silence. Finally breaking the uncomfortable silence, a person raised his hand and asked if I was an actor and how I got into that. I realized, not only by their silence but also from the looks on their faces and this off-topic question, that they were too afraid and uncomfortable to open up. There are a great many issues and topics that come up following my presentation, which I usually cover by fielding questions from the audience; here, I wound up going over all my main points without them asking any relevant questions.

The show—using the principles of intergroup contact theory—typically creates a safe enough environment for people to open up and tell their stories. In this room on this day, however, the audience all perceived the story as one primarily about race—they had recently experienced some harsh racial incidents at the plant, and thus the reason I was brought in. They knew coming in that race was going to be the topic we were exploring that day, and I sensed they were apprehensive about talking about it. There were three Black people, five women, a man who identified himself as Puerto Rican (although I wasn't sure about him until he actually identified), an Asian guy, and one Brit. I had engaged in some good conversations with quite a few people just before we started the session, and they seemed well aware of the content of the workshop before they arrived. Their reluctance, or rather fear, played out once they were asked to open up and talk. The training facilitators then moved slowly into the next phase of the workshop, building on the themes of trust, respect, and recognition of uncomfortable fear in having these conversations. As the session progressed, the group began to share bits of themselves with one another and to open up. At one point there was an exploration that resulted in a great conversation about early messages they received around race and how they came to see themselves framed in the history of this messaging.

By the end of the day we had witnessed a heartfelt open conversation between two line supervisors. One was a tough, hard-looking White woman dressed in soiled coveralls who had a leg disability about which she confessed feeling ashamed. The other, a tall young Black man in similar attire, spoke about growing up and always feeling or being treated as if he was a second-class citizen. He spoke calmly and frankly of his teenage years when he and his friends were repeatedly stopped by police for no apparent reason. He mentioned attending a nearly all-Black school even though a majority-White school was actually closer to home. He then admitted to the room that as a Black man he was very conscious of conducting himself in the manner he knew to be most successful with people who he understood saw him distinctly as a Black man: he was always on time, never angry, sometimes cautious, always courteous, and, most important, always trying to give 200 percent. The people in the room were quite taken by his story. His fellow line supervisor confessed to seeing him merely as her friend and coworker, but not necessarily as Black. As we pointed out the difference between her perception of her coworker and his story, she seemed to really understand the importance of learning this information about him. We talked about the negative effects of color blindness and how it related to her own visible disability, and she made the connection about the importance of both seeing and acknowledging what's in front of you and, more importantly, asking about one's story in order to understand more.

Later an assistant plant manager, an older White man who had been dialoguing with this same Black worker, pointed out that he remembered how difficult it was being a supervisor himself. He never imagined the added pressure of being a person of color and how that could impact the dynamic between workers. Another woman in the room—also a line worker in coveralls—confessed that whenever she heard the phrase "White privilege," it always made her angry, thinking she'd worked hard to get to where she was. But through the dialogue that day she began to see the issue in a new and different light—how other factors beyond her control were creating an unfair playing field where just working hard was not enough. Then the plant manager got up and told a story about living and working for the company in Malaysia. He remembered going to a mall with his family and being stared at and pointed to by the locals since his family were the only White people around. He never felt threatened, he said, like perhaps some feel here in the United States, but he was very aware of being different. He expressed how at the time he was embarrassed for his family.

It was fascinating that the phrase "White privilege" came up during the session. The facilitators and I had introduced the concept of privilege, but I don't remember anyone actually using the term *White*. Sometimes the omission is purposeful, as "White privilege" is another topic that can raise the temperature in the room for some people. The way this particular woman spoke about it was terrific, admitting the phrase was one that had irked her in the past and then acknowledging that hearing someone's story, a person she worked with and had a great deal of respect for, changed the way she heard the words.

In the end we had created an opening that started with the uncomfortableness of my show and my story and developed into a space where people, one by one, could open up and talk about what they were thinking. As we wrapped up for the day I could see that people in the group seemed lighter, more open and receptive to hearing and telling more of their own stories.

✳ ✳ ✳ ✳

Get comfortable being uncomfortable. Why would I want to do that? Who *wants* to be uncomfortable? In the theater world where my roots lie, this is an axiom that many abide by. The most dynamic, real, truthful work onstage is found when an actor is uncomfortable, unsure where his emotions will lead him from one moment to the next. It is widely touted in improvisation circles, since the actual doing of improv requires the actor to make it up on the fly in response to what one is given. If you can't get comfortable not knowing what is coming next, then acting and improv is probably not for you.

But in the real world, most folks like to have a little more consistency and knowledge about what to expect. You may not know exactly how your day will play out, but most people have a routine: they know what time they have to be at work, generally what their workday will entail, and what routes they'll probably be traveling.

Truthfully, however, we don't really expect most things that happen over the course of a day, not to mention, of course, the numerous curveballs thrown our way. The sheer act of a conversation—with a colleague at work, a family member, a neighbor, the bagger at the grocery store—is in fact an improvisation. Initially I may know what I want to ask or what I want to tell someone, but I don't actually know the answer nor quite how I will respond.

With that in mind, if we can get through our days navigating all that life haphazardly throws in our path, we can certainly commit to doing the same with a conversation about race and identity. What might frighten many of us is how little we actually know about others' identities and thus we hesitate to embark on a conversation. What if we were to lean into the discomfort and admit we know nothing? Perhaps that would be a good place to start!

It seems altogether likely that white people in the United States will continue to reassure themselves with black images derived from the folklore of white supremacy and the fakelore of black pathology so long as segregation enables them to ignore the actualities. They can afford such self-indulgence only because they carefully avoid circumstances that would require a confrontation with their own contradictions.

ALBERT MURRAY
THE OMNI AMERICANS

TOOL

Get comfortable being uncomfortable.

ACTION

Take the risk of talking about something you may feel uncomfortable about or have never discussed.

STARTING POINTS

- Acknowledge right off the top your discomfort or inexperience with talking about a particular topic. By saying it out loud you are helping others understand where you are coming from, and dissipating your own fear.

- Recognize that a conversation is an improvisation. You don't know what others are going to say nor how you will respond. We make it up as we go along, and we do it all the time!

SIX

Understand There Are Realities Outside Your Own Experience

Dear American Non-Black, if an American Black person is telling you about an experience about being black, please do not eagerly bring up examples from your own life. Don't say "It's just like when I . . ." You have suffered. Everyone in the world has suffered. But you have not suffered precisely because you are an American Black. Don't be quick to find alternative explanations for what happened. Don't say "Oh, it's not really race, it's class. Oh, it's not race, it's gender. Oh, it's not race, it's the cookie monster." You see, American Blacks actually don't WANT it to be race. They would rather not have racist shit happen. So maybe when they say something is about race, it's maybe because it actually is?

CHIMAMANDA NGOZI ADICHIE
AMERICANAH

J ust because we may not have experienced racism, sexism, homophobia, age discrimination, disability indifference, or other forms of discriminatory treatment, doesn't mean these are not realities for other people. We need to listen with empathy.

At a prestigious Northeastern boarding school—another of the top five private boarding schools in the country—during a workshop a young White female student was disturbed and hesitant when she disagreed about the presence of racism and White privilege in society. Following the election of Barack Obama—seen by many as proof that racism had been eliminated and now referred to as our postracial moment—she didn't believe racism was still such a big problem, and she took exception with the idea that White people had benefits (privileges) that didn't exist for Blacks. Her response was labored and her voice became almost a whisper. When challenged by other students in the class, both White and Black (two were present in the room out of a total of twenty-five), she backed off and refused to continue, visibly uncomfortable. I was careful not to let this become an overheated exchange with the opposing side pushing far stronger against her opinions. It is important for all experiences and ideas to be heard in a way that is respectful.

A Black student related a personal story about feeling slighted and not fully accepted in this school, which is predominantly White. He mentioned being excluded from groups that should have been accepting of his accomplishments and both the frustration and embarrassment this caused him. A White student then talked about seeing the difference in how she was treated versus a Black friend while the two were shopping at a large department store in New York City. There were conversations around these two experiences and a general sense of agreement that differences in treatment did exist.

Following the workshop I approached the young woman who had had the courage to speak out expressing her contrary opinion. I thanked her for expressing her opinion and participating in the dialogue. She was still uncomfortable but slightly relieved to receive my words of encouragement. I told her that even though she felt differently than perhaps most of her classmates, it is a vital part of our society to be able to discuss openly and respectfully issues that affect us all. While I and several of her classmates may not have agreed with her, it is important for her to express these thoughts in order for us all to be challenged and perhaps changed by what we hear. It was an uncomfortable moment, one in which it was difficult for some to see another person's reality. This young woman was unaware, blind to the ongoing racism and discrimination occurring at her own school.

* * * *

In the fall of 2013 I was asked to give a presentation for a judges' association in suburban Chicago. Following the presentation, I engaged the roomful of justices in a lively discussion about race and identity in their courtrooms. They couldn't seem to wrap their heads around the variety of cultural differences that appeared before them every day. Many misjudged what they perceived as disrespectful behavior from folks with poor language skills or cultural differences. Language barriers can make comprehension of difficult legal terms and concepts overwhelming, if not impossible without good and thorough translation. They perceived a defendant's inability to look up at them or their quietness as illogical behavior rather than as a cultural difference. For example, in some Latin cultures eye contact with strangers is nonexistent.

Many Black Americans also have distinct cultural differences when thrust into such a setting. A recent study showed that court reporters erred almost half the time in recording what is said by someone speaking a distinctive Black street vernacular. The television series *The Wire* provides an authentic taste of the difficulties in parsing Black street vernacular.

An assumption by many in the room was that the defendant should be fully prepared (presumably by their mostly court-appointed attorneys or others) to cooperate on the judge's terms.

There was little comprehension of how intimidating it can be for an immigrant, for example, to try to speak or understand what is to them a foreign language in such a fraught setting. In the courtroom people rise to their feet as this person—the judge—dressed in a long, flowing black gown enters the room, sits down, and strikes a hammer loudly on a piece of wood. This is a scene many cannot relate to, let alone navigate burdened with vast cultural differences.

There was an expectation on the part of these justices that people should know exactly how to behave in the courtroom even though for many it may be their first time in such a setting and a reality with which they are completely unfamiliar.

* * * *

During the Ferguson protests that took place following the killing of an unarmed young Black man by a police officer, I happened to catch a panel discussion on FOX News. It was on Eric Bolling's show, and the panel consisted of a young White woman whose bio said she was a media expert, an older White man who was a financial investor (and a former actor on the old *M.A.S.H.* television series), and a younger White man who was also some kind of an investment expert. They were discussing why they thought—given their expertise in this area—that race was not what the Ferguson incident was about. That the young dead Black man was a criminal was the reason he was killed, and thus the incident was one about crime and not race. At one point the younger White man on the panel was asked about the inherent racism of the Black protesters, and he said, "The only people talking about race are racists."

* * * *

After a workshop on identity at a private school in Chicago, a young woman approached me as I was exiting the classroom and pulled me aside in private. She expressed her deep appreciation for the work I was doing and about how my play (which I had performed early in the day for the entire school) had had a powerful impact on her. She confessed she was in transition from male to female and that she felt so outside of everyone and everything at the school. She admitted she didn't feel threatened or unsafe, but the confusion and intolerance she experienced was often depressing. Classmates couldn't understand or wrap their heads (let alone arms!) around her reality, and they acted out inappropriately without thought at times.

She thought my story could perhaps be something that might help open the door on conversations about other people's realities. She took away from the show and the workshop a sense that one doesn't always have to be comfortable, or make people comfortable in their own discomfort.

* * * *

I visited the corporate offices of a financial services company near Chicago in the fall of 2015 and did a presentation for a group of about 350. The response was terrific and the talkback quite engaging. During the talkback, a woman who was formerly a French citizen and who had recently converted to Islam spoke about her transition not only from France to America but also of her experience here and in France of wearing a head scarf. She talked about becoming acutely aware of how people began to look at her differently once she started wearing the hijab. She lamented her journey from acceptance to rejection, from being virtually unseen to being stared at and vilified. It was a stark reminder of what the simple gesture of covering one's head can provoke. I commented on how, as Americans, we needed to be more accepting and, in regard to my own transformative experience, how it changed the way I viewed being half White.

Four days following that presentation, I received the following email:

> Took a few days to digest the play and the discussion afterward . . . the play itself and your acting was outstanding.
>
> Your comments afterward, however, hit me as racist and race baiting . . . particularly your comment "my experience might have changed how I see white people."
>
> Really? All white people? That's a pretty broad generalization about an entire race, most of whom you've never met, which is pretty much the definition of racism.
>
> Now I have learned from living in Chicago that I should not engage young black men because they are the group most likely to shoot you, based on statistics. 3 women robbed at gunpoint one block from my front door at 8 a.m. in 1 day makes this indisputable . . .
>
> That's not racism, it's common sense. But you'll call it racism, because it fits your message . . . which is that even though most white people would never harm you, you can still hate them in general for what they never personally did to anyone . . . and that even though as a race, black people are quite dangerous where I live, I shouldn't treat them differently than white people, even though there are no white people shooting at each other in Chicago.
>
> Your message is silly and biased, and I will file it under lowbrow entertainment.
>
> I hope the first amendment protects me when I tell to [sic] that I really believe your divisive message has no place anywhere in society, much less at work. Shame on you for spreading garbage like that.

I sat staring at my computer screen stunned. I was unsure exactly how I should feel or even react. I'd never received a response of this kind. It was so incomprehensible to me that I thought perhaps I was being trolled or punked or someone was playing a prank. It wasn't even clear to me whether this person was in the audience of my recent visit to the financial services firm, or saw me somewhere else. I was also terribly disturbed by this person's response and their accusations about my feelings toward White people. I certainly had not said, or even tried to imply, what the writer of the email suggested. It was outrageous and frankly ridiculous, I thought. I was being misinterpreted and needed to set the record straight.

If I were to respond, I thought an email would not be the most effective method. Emails (even letters for that matter) and social media (Facebook, Twitter, etc.) do not constitute dialogue, certainly not in any constructive way. However, I did feel the need to respond and wanted to do so in a respectful manner, no matter how offensive I found this person's response to my show and post-show dialogue.

As I began to consider this person's thoughts more carefully, I realized not only that this person was brave, but that I was somewhat happy they had written. How many times have we stifled our response to something and not shared our truth? In some cases our dishonesty in this regard is a means to protect someone from harm or hurt, but in many situations the truth is exactly what should be shared, yet isn't.

I wrote the person back, thanking them for their courage and honesty in writing. I admitted I thought at first they were trolling me—I have had that happen in the past—but welcomed their safety in writing. I did qualify my response by pointing out that I believe true dialogue only happens face to face, but that I understood why this may have been difficult in front of all those colleagues.

I then let the writer know that I was disturbed by their characterization of my "new" attitude toward White people. In no uncertain terms was I implying that all White people are racist. I am half White, I pointed out, half my family is White, my wife is White—how could I think they were racist? In a similar way I made reference to the Glenn Beck comment about President Obama's hatred for White people and how ridiculous that is, since he is half White and was raised by Whites.

I suggested the conclusion that all Black men should not be engaged is essentially the same thing the writer accuses me of—using a broad brush is the definition of racism—and that it is false to suggest that most White men wouldn't harm you or that White people aren't shooting at people from time to time. I implied that there are different realities and that we need to be more accepting of other people's experiences which may be different from our own (even hers to mine!). I reiterated my belief that writing cannot serve as dialogue and wrote that, if they felt comfortable, I would be happy to meet them in person somewhere to their liking to talk face to face. Finally, in an attempt to lighten the mood a bit, I addressed the contradiction concerning my show:

> What confuses me about your comment is that in the opening you state, "the play itself and your acting was outstanding," but by the end you suggest you will file it under lowbrow entertainment. Which is it?

Later that day I got another quick response, equally distressing as the first one. This is just a portion of what the person wrote:

> The writing and acting and the story itself were spellbinding . . . deeply moving, but in the discussion it seemed like you used that same emotion to make most white people look like racists. I know you are aware that many black families don't want their children dating white people either . . . you were very lucky that your black family was raised better. But I never see anyone acknowledging that black racism against white people exists, even though I feel it every day with dirty looks and frowns from black parents when I smile at their children . . . and this happened to me in San Francisco as often as it happens here in Chicago.
> I don't care what color or orientation or how fat or skinny somebody is as long as they support themselves if able and don't

blame others for their failures. It's been a really long time since slavery, my Irish roots include indentured servants . . . I just am of the mind that because U.S. taxpayers have provided free housing and education and food and medical care to people, they should have been able to make positive changes in their families . . . I'm dismayed at gangs and people who seem hell bent on living in a war zone. It looks like a choice more than it looks like oppression from my Chicago angle.

The writer made mention that they didn't mean to call my show "lowbrow" and that they liked it very much, so much so that they would like to see it again. However, this person made clear they would skip the talkback portion. The email ended with another total misconception that blew my mind:

> My real logical question I would ask if I had no fear of repercussions is "why do people stay in the ghetto? It seems dirty and dangerous, and your cha voucher is good in the nicer parts of town or the state with better schools and grocery stores and fewer shootings? Why do you segregate yourselves to that part of the world?"

Once again I stared incomprehensively at my screen, trying to process what I was reading. Even though I found this new response even more disturbing than the first, I again became aware of the fact that this is actually how some people view the world. This is someone's reality, and if I am to suggest that we all must accept others' realities, then I needed to wrap my head around this one. At first, I made an attempt to talk some truth to what I perceived as mistruths, but in the end I decided that, without actually sitting down face to face, I couldn't really take this any further, if there was any further to go!

I simply replied with my thanks and wished them well.

❄ ❄ ❄ ❄

After a set of presentations at a government agency I received the following email note addressing a very different reality:

Yesterday I was on the video production team supporting the webcast of your show and regrettably wasn't able to ask the following questions in person. As a Christian, I was taken aback by your twice use [*sic*] of the name of Jesus Christ as an exclamation during your performance. I wonder, is that language an intentional part of your script? And if so, have you considered how your use of Jesus' name in such a flippant manner might needlessly offend your Christian audience? Do you think it is appropriate during a diversity and inclusion event aimed at engendering commonality to use language so marginalizing toward Christians?

In all the years, after hundreds, close to a thousand shows, only twice before had anyone ever addressed this issue. The first time was after a show at an extremely conservative Catholic high school where the multicultural director at the school implied the language might have been inappropriate for the students, but he thought the overall message outweighed the infraction. Nonetheless, he suggested that in the future I should inform schools before I let things fly, so they can decide whether the language is appropriate for their student body. The second time was after a corporate presentation in the Pacific Northwest, where an older woman approached me privately and suggested my use of *Jesus* was akin to using the N-word.

Again, I was appreciative of this person for writing and felt I could respond in a respectful manner. I thanked them and suggested it was not my intention to offend, nor were the words *Jesus* and *God* used by the characters in my play in a sacrilegious manner. My grandmother, whom I quote using the word God, was in fact a deeply religious person and a proud long-standing member of her church. My father, who exclaimed, "Jesus Christ," upon seeing me for the first time, was simply expressing shock by using that phrase. These were both direct quotes from my family members, actually captured on video. I also pointed out that my show was originally directed (as well as shaped) with the aid of a director who also happens to be a lay minister of his church.

Finally I pointed out that this is the very thing I am trying to address:

> Again, I am sorry you were offended, but I would like to venture that there were perhaps other Christians in the room that day. And perhaps some of those Christians were as offended as you, but I am guessing that not all of them were. Would you think that a reasonable estimation? If so, I suggest that this is the very thing I am trying to address . . . . that Christians, like Blacks, or Whites, or adopted people (or gay people, or any other group you may want to insert here) are not a monolith. That is, each are individuals in those respective groups, and therefore not all will respond in the same way. HOWEVER, as a society, this is how we/they are judged . . . as all being the same within a certain group.

I concluded by mentioning the many churches and religious-based schools I have performed for and how only once did I ever get a comment about the language. That is not to say that there may not have been some folks at these places who didn't feel the same way as he did; it is just to point out that they didn't allow any offense with the language to get in the way of the overall message.

✳ ✳ ✳ ✳

After a presentation for a group of teachers at a public high school in the western suburbs of Chicago, a White teacher (as were a majority that afternoon) recognized the difficulties my mother experienced in trying to navigate a racial divide between her parents, society, and her own beliefs. The teacher said she was sensitive to some of her students' attempts to forge conversations about what they perceived as inequalities when many of their peers did not see or understand what they were referring to. She thought the similarity, even though some fifty years apart, was a rich example of both how difficult it is to talk about it and the difference in perceptions between races regarding discrimination.

Suddenly another teacher (White) broke in, shaking her head in disagreement. "I don't think we acknowledge the amount of racism against Whites," she chided. "There's plenty of discrimination I feel that goes unnoticed."

"You feel you're being discriminated against?" I asked half innocently, half incredulously.

"Yes," she said, "I feel we don't recognize racism against Whites."

"You feel, as a White person, that you experience racism?" I asked her to clarify.

"Yes, I do. I think there's too much focus on the Black kids," she pointed out bluntly. "I don't feel like anyone recognizes how we spend too much time talking about them, and no time talking about us," she laid out to the now deadly silent room.

I took in her opinions calmly and slowly looked across the room. I could feel a general uncomfortableness, but there was no effort to combat this teacher's words. I couldn't tell if it was because this woman was a bit of a bully whom the other teachers feared, or if there was an underlying fear about opening up and engaging in this much needed, but extremely uncomfortable, conversation. Or perhaps this woman had a reputation for being a bit of a nut, who knows?!

I thanked her for her thoughts and pointed out it was important for all voices to be heard. If this was indeed the way she truly felt, then it was a reality that needed to be discussed. However, I also suggested that if one were to look around the room or in classrooms, the reality is that there is a minority of students of color at their school. Therefore the default, the norm, is White. Often the norm does not get as much discussion since it is what is accepted as the starting point for everything. We often don't identify people or things as White when it is the norm (and the overwhelming majority in many places), but we do identify people or things as Black.

As for discrimination, I suggested she might want to think about how that really plays itself out in her life or in the lives of the White students. I asked her, since the Black student population at this school hovers around 3 percent (I'd been told this in conversations before I'd arrived to do my work), in what kinds of things are you personally disadvantaged? Have you had to take a pay cut or been demoted? Have your White students suffered a disadvantage in disciplinary actions or obtaining spots in AP classes or in graduation rates? What specifically do you think is happening that leads you to the conclusion that there is racism against Whites at your school? I then suggested she needn't answer me right now but to think it over and talk with her colleagues. I could tell the room, still quietly uncomfortable, was somewhat relieved but also hesitant. Would they now have to have this conversation with their colleague? Or was her reality theirs as well?

* * * *

As I write this there has been a string of countless incidents reported in which people of color have been humiliated, harassed, and even arrested for simply being present in a particular place where for others it is completely accepted. Two Black men were arrested at a Starbucks for sitting and waiting for a White colleague to arrive. A group of Black people were questioned by police as they were leaving an Airbnb, which they had just checked out of, after a White neighbor thinking they were criminals called the cops. Two young Black men were accused of shoplifting at a Nordstrom after a White salesclerk followed them and a White customer harassed them by calling them punks, and yet no shoplifting had taken place. Two young Native American boys, arriving late for a tour of a college campus in Colorado, were reported by a White member of the tour as being "creepy" and "suspicious" and were subsequently detained by police. A Black graduate student at Yale who fell asleep in a common area in her dorm was questioned by police after a

White resident of the dorm reported her as "suspicious." All these incidents happened in the first two weeks of May 2018.

When we hear stories like these, do we distrust them because we do not know these people? Do we think these are just random incidents that rarely happen? Why would we doubt these other experiences? Because they are not a part of our own experience? Why would the experience of another person who looks, sounds, or acts differently than us be questioned as false, fabricated, or an act?

If you are not Black, how can you possibly know what it is like to walk around as a Black person? Likewise as a gay person? Or Asian? Or (fill in the other)? And why would you assume Black people (and others not like you) are fabricating discriminatory experiences? Those who are other are too sensitive, is what some suggest. "Slavery happened a long time ago. Get over it!" To which I would suggest reading more history; we've never really reckoned with our past, and many are not getting the fuller picture that's slowly emerging. Some might say, "It doesn't matter if you're Black or White, gay or straight, we're all human beings and there is no difference." To that I suggest, we are all different: I am still firmly in the camp that believes we have more in common than we are different. Yet, we are all different in some way. Starting at our roots, we can recognize we all have differences between ourselves and our parents, between ourselves and a sibling—differences in gender, age, or interests—they are real and they exist. The manager who shared his experience of being stared at as the sole White person at a mall in Malaysia was cognizant of the big difference his Whiteness represented.

This may be one of *the* most difficult tasks for many people in this ongoing conversation. How do I actually put myself in someone else's shoes? What would that look like? How would that feel? Much like the unconscious biases we all have in regards to various people or things, and the inherent difficulty of uncovering what those biases might be, the acceptance of other people's realities is in this same strain. If I am not Black, how can I possibly know what it is like to live as a Black person? And to further complicate things, this question presumes that all Black people live the same way—which they don't! If I am not gay, how could I possibly know what it would be like to be gay? Again, this seems to presume all gay people are the same! It goes on and on, but regardless, we must listen, we must remain open and willing to learn about one another's life issues.

All people are both the objects and the perpetrators of prejudice. Our understanding of the prejudice directed against us informs our responses to others.
ANDREW SOLOMON
FAR FROM THE TREE

TOOL
Understand there are realities outside of your own experience. Just because we may not have personally experienced racism, sexism, homophobia, age discrimination, disability indifference, or other forms of discriminatory treatment, doesn't mean these are not realities for other people. We need to listen with empathy.

ACTION
Put yourself in someone else's shoes.

STARTING POINTS
- Make a list of all the names you have ever been called—both good and bad—and write about how each one affected you.
- In a small group, discuss what it means to be an American, then talk about all the different ways we define that.
- In a small group, talk about the early messages you were given about gender, sexuality, and disabilities.

SEVEN

Practice Forgiveness

If we want to reduce inequalities and injustices and racial, ethnic, religious and other tensions, the only reasonable and decent policy is to work to ensure that every citizen is treated as a fully-fledged member of society, whatever his affiliations. Of course, such a destination cannot be reached from one day to the next, but that is no reason for driving in the opposite direction.

AMIN MAALOUF
*IN THE NAME OF IDENTITY:
VIOLENCE AND THE NEED TO BELONG*

In the spring of 2014 I was invited by the faculty of arts and sciences at an Ivy League college for a second time to speak as a part of their series Difficult Dialogues. I was thrilled to be asked to speak again at such a prestigious institution of higher learning. I am proud to say I was the only speaker to be asked to present twice during the five years of this series' existence. However, this time they asked if I would lead a workshop on unconscious bias and cultural competency.

For weeks I worked on the format for the day, hoping to stir people up and get them conversing with one another, rather than having me do most of the talking. I worked with the Office of Human Resources on creating a program that would push people's boundaries and get them to think about things they rarely talk about: race, identity, stereotypes, unconscious bias, and cultural competency. The college sent a schedule in advance; the day was to begin with comments by a highly respected and much lauded writer and professor from the school, leading into his introduction of my work and biographical details.

Although some in attendance had seen me perform my play on campus a couple years prior when I was first invited to participate in Difficult Dialogues, I began the workshop with an abbreviated version of the story to find my biological father. It was important to put things in context as to why I was there, my relationship to the topics, and the importance of utilizing personal story as a means to find common ground. As usual, the retelling of my story engaged folks in laughter as well as deep thought, which was evident in the questions the participants peppered me with.

Utilizing the Q&A as a springboard into a more interactive section of the session allowed people to open up, engage with one another, and share things in what they now perceived as a safe environment. As I guided the group of 160-plus people (many more than I would ideally like to work with), I observed a number of people's apprehensions turn to joyful discoveries as they shared personal anecdotes about one another. They broke down barriers of difference and found commonalities in sharing personal stories. Over the course of the two hours people became unguarded, allowing them to be vulnerable and dig deeper into their shared histories.

We ended the workshop with an uplifting story from a participant who was initially uncomfortable with the idea of talking about perceptions of people and how we arrived at them. However, once she leaned into the uncomfortableness, she found herself opening up with a new colleague, and they effortlessly discovered things they had in common.

As people filed out, several approached and thanked me for opening the door on these type of conversations at their institution (which, many confessed during the workshop, had at times seemed very disinterested in this type of programming and training). A few inquired as to where they could purchase my book (I usually have them available, but here there was a campus policy that forbids outside speakers from selling on campus), and more than a few encouraged me to return and lead further explorations on race and identity.

Several months later, the Human Resources Department sent me the results of the post-workshop survey they conducted. They were very pleased by the response. The results indicated that 82 percent of those surveyed felt strongly positive about the session, with about 13 percent neutral. That left about 5 percent of those surveyed disliking the session. I guess I never thought about the fact that you really can't please all the people all the time, but to see that there were those who felt dissatisfied was disheartening. I read though the comments people shared and was struck quite haltingly by one particular negative comment: *Mr. Fosberg is an actor, not a facilitator. I was surprised to see him in this role. He was not an expert, and it showed.*

The bluntness of this person's comment hit me hard. Knowing full well this was just one person's opinion, and that a majority of people that day (at least those who filled out surveys) were very pleased and satisfied with my efforts, it still hurt a great deal. I mentally began to run through all the diversity work I'd done over the years. Sure, I was acting out my story in play form and was indeed a trained actor, but by this point I had facilitated dialogues at hundreds of locations with a wide variety of people. I had also consumed articles, essays, news stories, books, films, and panel discussions—literally everything I could get my hands on that dealt with race and identity issues. I'd worked with other diversity and inclusion trainers, collaborating on programs to help corporate teams open up and dialogue. I'd been to conferences, written articles and blog posts, and spoken to a variety of media outlets on these topics as well. I found I wanted to talk to the person who wrote this comment and defend my qualifications. I was hurt and now also angry.

Then I remembered something that might have been a factor in this person's perception. When the folks in Human Resources at the college had asked me to send a bio (which the esteemed professor read following his opening remarks before my program), I had provided one that spoke more about my qualifications as an actor, using the play as a diversity tool. It did not address all the specific work I had engaged in within the diversity and inclusion sphere. So this was the first impression many of the participants had of me: an actor who answers questions following his play.

I then had a moment of enormous clarity: I realized an unconscious bias of my own, a bias that, although simple, was based on first (limited) impressions. Ever since I was in high school I have been going to the theater to see plays. Over the course of my lifetime I have seen hundreds, perhaps thousands of shows, from Broadway to off Broadway to the storefronts of Chicago's thriving theater scene. The routine, as for many a theatergoer, is that when I arrive at the theater I am handed a program as I walk into the theater. I find my seat, open the program before the curtain rises, and begin to read the bios of the actors in that evening's performance. As I read each bio, I am mentally judging the actors on their qualifications: this one went to Carnegie Mellon (a highly overrated theater school in my opinion), that one was in such and such a play (I hated that play), this one had a role in some TV drama (as if television is legit!). I am judging the actors before they even step out onto the stage!

Recalling this was a stark reminder at how pernicious biases can be and how even those who think they are unaffected by bias have much work to do. From that day forward I stopped reading programs before plays I attend. As a trained actor I may still be more discerning than the average theatergoer, but I can say I have enjoyed watching theater more since I've stopped making initial judgments about the actors in the shows.

In this way I felt that not only did I need to forgive the person for the survey comment made following my visit to this prestigious ivy league school, but perhaps indeed I needed to thank them. More important, however, I needed to forgive myself for overlooking my own bias. This incident made me aware—the first step in making change—and allowed me to begin tackling my own preconceived notions. Realizing how easy it is to prejudge someone or to have expectations about something has helped me slow my process down. Upon meeting a new person am I judging them on what they are wearing or perhaps what I've been told about them? Or am I allowing them to make their own impression upon me? In the lead-up to doing something, am I prejudging what I expect to have happen or am I in the moment when I am there?

* * * *

In my play, my story, the moment of forgiveness occurs when my friend Tommy calls and offers me a bit of advice regarding the anger I held toward my mother for not telling me about my biological father. Tommy helped me see how difficult it must have been for my mother in the late 1950s, having been raised by proud immigrant parents. Much like many of today's immigrants to America, they wanted their daughter to marry one of their own. The fact that my mother had a child with and then married a Black man was completely unacceptable to her parents, as it may still be for many immigrant families as well as American families with less connection to their immigrant past. The shame and guilt my mother was forced to endure was not all of her own making. In my phone conversation with Tommy, he suggested the gift of understanding and forgiveness. By coming to an understanding of the pressures she felt, it would allow me to forgive her. This act of forgiveness could then help us move on and forge a path of reconciliation.

His advice also helped me understand, in a broader sense, the damage caused by hanging on to resentment and anger. When we operate from a place of anger or resentment, we cannot think clearly. Our thoughts and actions are clouded by these emotions, and we tend to respond in unhealthful, not to mention unhelpful, ways. Stop and think about all the anger currently being stirred up and how that anger and resentment has fomented acts of violence. The anti-Semitic mass shooting at a synagogue in Pittsburgh in 2018 and the Unite the Right rally in Charlottesville in 2017 are just two incidents that resulted in deaths perpetrated by American's stirred up anger and resentment. The harassment, bullying, and rough acts committed at presidential rallies during the last election have roots in this anger. Instead of rallying us to find our better angels and embrace things that can unite us all, President Trump has rallied those with already simmering pots to act out, such as the deranged man in Florida who sent pipe bombs to Democratic politicians, journalists, and a prominent Jewish financier. These calls or rallies to action take advantage of what the Chinese study discovered about anger contagion online (see chapter 4); we are more drawn to anger than we are to joy, and it feeds upon itself, creating more.

What role can forgiveness play?

✳ ✳ ✳ ✳

When I set out to publish my memoir in 2008, I discovered not only how complicated the publishing world is, but once again the lessons of recognizing that there are many different ways to talk about race and, ultimately, that forgiveness would allow me to forge ahead with my message.

I had been introduced to an editor who worked for a university press. She became intrigued by my story and the work I was doing to finish a manuscript for a memoir. We mapped out a strategy for completing the text and discussed how we might proceed to publication. I was really excited about the possibility of finding a publisher since I had heard many stories about the difficulties of finding a home for literary work that were filled with sad endings.

As I continued to work on the manuscript over the ensuing months, my editor left the university press and wound up becoming an acquisitions manager for a larger, notable independent publisher. I assumed our deal was dead but she informed me she was bringing me along with her in the transition. The new deal came with better terms—I got an advance—and the publisher had greater resources to distribute and promote the book. It looked like a win-win as far as I was concerned!

It was difficult to carve out time to write; my touring schedule and managing all that went with it could be overwhelming at times. I generally found myself constantly on the road from mid-January (leading up to Martin Luther King Day and through February, which is Black History Month) up to the beginning of April. I was exceedingly grateful for the many opportunities to perform and facilitate meaningful dialogues, but trying to squeeze in writing was not something that came naturally to me. I managed to squeeze out editing time and finished my draft by late spring 2008, nervously handing it over to the publishers by early June that year.

It wasn't until nearly the end of 2008 when my new publisher called and requested I change the title of the book. Up to that point, the only title I'd considered, the only one that even made sense to me, was the same as the title of my one-man play, *Incognito*. *Incognito* is defined in the dictionary as "with the real identity concealed, with one's identity hidden or unknown." Not only did that word encapsulate exactly my predicament, but as a title for the memoir, it also reflected the connection to the play, which I was now performing fifty plus times a year. I knew I could sell copies of the book after presentations, and it made sense to me to maintain consistency in branding, a word I'd heard bandied about in successful companies and a very hot concept at the time.

The publisher, on the other hand, thought the title was stupid, not sexy enough, unrecognizable, and they claimed it wouldn't sell books. They insisted I change it or—as they gently threatened—they would not invest any time or money into promotion or distribution. I would wind up selling the books all by myself after presentations. I consulted other writer friends, who suggested it might be better to compromise, so I relented and agreed to come up with new title suggestions.

After a couple days I submitted a half dozen new title ideas, but the publisher came back to me with a title they had come up with. They insisted theirs be the new title and sent me a cover concept complete with artwork. I took one look and my heart sank: *Suddenly Black: How a Phone Call Changed My Race.* I was terribly disappointed and felt trapped in an untenable position.

I couldn't help thinking about how I was both lucky to be in a position to actually write and publish my life story and yet terribly unhappy with the title I felt I was being forced to live with. If you get a chance to tell your life story, is that what you'd want to call it?! Yet, as my writer friends had professed, a publishing deal isn't easy to come by. I felt I should at least consider swallowing my pride and moving forward with publication.

I felt torn about the title in particular because it did not reflect the message I was trying to send about race and identity. "Suddenly Black" is not what I wanted to project into the discourse on race. I had not actually become suddenly Black; the transition and message are much more nuanced than that. And it wasn't just a phone call that changed the way I came to my newfound identity. If there is one thing I hope *my* experience shows here, it is that these topics are fraught with a wide variety of opinions. Not only is there not but one way to go about having a conversation about race and identity, there are so many different experiences, beliefs, opinions, and ideas that there isn't any consensus. Therefore, I believe great care must be taken when writing or talking about these topics. "Suddenly Black" was not careful or even thoughtful . . . it was in your face and stereotypical. It was promoting the idea that one can only be Black or White. It seemed cheap and perhaps overly sensational.

I did, however, swallow whatever pride I had left and reluctantly agree to move forward. Not long after that, just days after we rang in the New Year, I was preparing to go on my usual extended January–April tour schedule when the publisher reached out again. The spring 2009 publication date, which they'd chosen without informing me, was fast approaching. They needed to put this book on a fast track in order to include it in their catalogue for that spring, which had already been laid out. They had been sitting on the completed manuscript for about eight months with nary a sign anyone had yet to read it. But now, in the beginning of January, a new editor (a copy editor, a different person from the one I'd been working with) sent back the redacted document filled with changes and edits that challenged the actual content and distorted what I was trying to say.

This was the start of a contentious exchange. The copy editor had flagged all the unanswered questions I posed in the manuscript. She insisted that if I were to ask questions of the reader, I must also offer answers. So, she asked, *what are the answers?* I told her I did not know the answers and thus the reason I was asking the questions—to provoke the reader to look for answers themselves and to suggest that perhaps for many questions there is more than one answer.

She also felt I spent too much time talking about father/son relationships, which she found unimportant. At this point, I literally had to stop reading her notes. If this person—a woman—could not understand why a male writer who grew up without his biological father, a man who discovers he is a different race than the one he came to identify with, would want to delve into the great importance of his father/son/stepfather relationship, then I was done! And I told her so in an email I sent that afternoon.

I received a phone call the next day from the publisher, from yet another woman, who was disturbed by what she saw as my obstinate position. She quite understandably stood by her editor but refused to, or maybe couldn't, understand my point. She also found questions without answers troubling and thought the father/son issues were overblown. It occurred to me then that we had no future, which I may have told her was the case. She suggested we take some time to think it over and reconvene the following day. I was troubled that night, thinking I'd spent all this time trying to get my book published only for naught. I felt I'd wasted time and sales. The sooner I could get this thing completed, the more opportunity I had to share the broader story and issues with the public at large.

The next day, the publisher and I parted ways. They asked me to return the advance (it was a mere few thousand dollars), but I suggested they may want to speak to my attorney and gave his name and contact information. They did not call him. I needed to practice what my friend Tommy had taught me: forgive and move on. I couldn't afford nor did I want to hang on to the anger and resentment. The publisher and I saw the message of my book differently, and I needed to feel good about that, not resentful.

I ultimately decided to self-publish. It took another year and a half to complete the process since I was determined to produce a quality book that read great. I hired an independent editor and a book designer and included artwork from my sister. I released the finished product in February 2011 to coincide with Black History Month. It won a couple of independent publishing awards and was reviewed well in those publications that accept self-produced works (not many do). I decided to hire a publicist to help take advantage of media opportunities that could result from interest in my story.

In marketing my book, there were many lessons I walked away with when it came to dealing with the the media, but one that seemed to be most prevalent is the fact that they move at the speed of light. Everything happens so fast there is rarely time for reflection or second thoughts. Deadlines are not tomorrow, but last week, and extent of coverage is minuscule. Think sound bites treated as full-blown stories.

On the one hand, how news reporters stand up to this constant pace is impressive, on the other, it is sad and disappointing. Rarely does a story seem to get the coverage it needs to be fully understood, unless of course it's politics or an in-depth deep dive on a social problem. Another invaluable lesson when dealing with the media: forgiveness will allow for sanity!

My first experience with national media happened when CNN caught wind of my story (prior to publication of my memoir) and decided to do a long piece about me and the show. This happened during the lead-up to a special performance I was giving at Victory Gardens Theater in Chicago (a regional Tony Award–winning theater). A CNN producer found the whole story/play/dialogue-about-race idea fascinating and was assigned to do an in-depth piece.

The producer arrived along with a crew at my tiny apartment one afternoon, and we proceeded to spend a good portion of the day talking on camera. Next we walked up and down my street, capturing a casual-man-on-the-street interview. The following day I visited their studios in the Tribune Tower, giving another interview in the studio along with another man-on-the-street walk down Michigan Avenue. They then attended my performance that night and filmed a portion of the show along with the scintillating post-show talkback. After spending a couple days editing what must have been a great deal of footage, the producer informed me the piece was set to air the following Monday night. I was so excited I could barely contain myself. A major cable station was about to share my story and the work I was trying to promote, which had the potential to spread nationally. I called and emailed everyone I knew and gave them the air-date particulars.

I waited impatiently over the weekend, then that Monday the morning news broke that a Republican senator from Idaho by the name of Larry Craig had been arrested in the men's room at the Minneapolis airport in June for lewd behavior (that is, soliciting sex). For the next week the news was nonstop Larry Craig, partly because he'd been a

harsh critic of gay rights and partly because it was so salacious. My story was bumped to possibly Friday; however, by the end of the week the Larry Craig furor had yet to die down and the piece on my show was subsequently shelved and never saw the light of day. A gay antigay Republican was all the nation could talk about!

I held onto my anger over this for quite some time. I couldn't believe the news (and general public?) was so fixated on salaciousness that they would bump a positive story. I stayed stuck in that resentment for quite some time, and it colored everything I did in relationship to the media until the publication of my book. By the time the book came out, I had learned a few more lessons—or I should say, a few more lessons became very apparent to me—which helped me let go and move forward with my work and the necessity of dealing with the media. I committed to accepting who they are and what they are capable of (and not), and I remained committed to the work of helping people discover commonalities. I cannot change everyone's mind-set about race and identity, just like I cannot control what the media does or does not cover when it comes to my work. Forgiveness allowed me to move past them and dig deeper into my role as a bridge.

It is important to note that you can forgive someone yet not condone their actions. It may be difficult to reconcile this, but just because we forgive someone does not mean we also condone their behavior. However, holding on to resentment is in essence holding on to anger and keeps us from moving on. Anger and hatred is a prison, it grips us and keeps us in that spot persistently. While we carry anger, resentment, or hostility inside us, we can never find common ground with which to discover our many, many connections. Our commonalities are in abundance, and yet it is in the few differences that we allow ourselves to be driven apart.

I have walked that long road to freedom. I have tried not to falter; I have made missteps along the way. But I have discovered the secret that after climbing a great hill, one only finds that there are many more hills to climb. I have taken a moment here to rest, to steal a view of the glorious vista that surrounds me, to look back on the distance I have come. But I can rest only for a moment, for with freedom come responsibilities, and I dare not linger, for my long walk is not yet ended.

NELSON MANDELA
LONG WALK TO FREEDOM

TOOL

Practice forgiveness. It has been described as the hardest work you will ever do, but the most rewarding.

ACTION

Forgiving is an act of selflessness. Let go of anger and resentment.

STARTING POINT

Before you forgive others, it is often helpful to forgive one's self. Make amends where necessary, establish clear boundaries, and let go of anger.

EIGHT

Incognito: The Script

Copyright © 2000, Michael S. Fosberg

The first rehearsal for Incognito *took place on the morning of September 11, 2001, with the subsequent production taking place at the Bailiwick Theater, Chicago, opening October 17, 2001, with the following credits:*

Writer/Performer:	Michael S. Fosberg
Director:	Michael E. Myers
Set Designer:	Ryan McKinty-Trupp
Lighting Designer:	Tamora Wilson
Sound Designer:	Cecil Averett
Video Design:	Christopher Clepper
Stage Manager:	Don Bapst

Produced for Bailiwick Repertory by David Zak and Rusty Hernandez.

It was subsequently produced at the Apple Tree Theater in Highland Park, Illinois, February 13 – March 17, 2002.

That was followed up with a production at the Missouri Repertory Theatre (now Kansas City Rep) in September, 2002.

NOTE: The following script has been edited down over the years from the original two-hour production to what you see here on the page, which is approximately fifty minutes.

[A laptop computer sits on a desk center stage. There are chairs set across the stage, each representing a geographic area.

Music comes up: track I, "The Unbreakable Chain. Michael steps onstage, crosses to desk, and stands. Music fades out.]

I left Los Angeles aboard my sturdy sport utility vehicle at 7 a.m. on a typically bright sunny morning. A road trip . . . .

However, I wasn't just going on a trip across the country alone. I was, as I told friends and family, going to write a book. A book on finding myself and my family. The mission was to drive West coast to East, stopping off along the way, interviewing each family member, and compiling the juicy revelations into book form. It didn't matter that I'd never written a book before and hadn't the slightest idea of where to start. The idea sounded so good . . . plus . . . I had a great story.

[types and says] "Incognito, by Michael Sidney Fosberg" . . . [pause for writer's block] Shit! . . . Chapter One . . . [begins typing as he says] The Valley . . . Exactly six years before I set out on my road trip odyssey, I found myself living in the foothills of the sun-baked, thick-aired San Fernando Valley.

I sat gazing out over the smog filled Valley one unemployed morning, when I got a call from my 25 going on five-year-old sounding sister in Chicago, Lora Beth, or B.

"Michael, It's me, B . . ."

"What's up B?"

"Mom and Dad are getting a divorce."

"What?"

"She's leaving him. She told me today."

"Leaving him? They've been married 25 years . . . it can't be that simple."

"She won't say . . . She's not talking."

❊ ❊ ❊ ❊

Three weeks later I was on a plane to Chicago.

"Oh Mikey, it's great to have you home honey."

"Good to be home Mom. How's *everything?*"

"Everything's fine honey. The house has really shaped up since last you were here." Referring to the brand new "dream home" they had recently built in the swanky Chicago suburb of Lake Forest.

"I can see that. Very nice . . ."

The morning I was to return to California, I found myself in a car driven by my mother through Waukegan where I'd grown up. I gazed out the window recalling my entire childhood history, while my mother drove us cautiously towards their home-soon-to-be-gone in the burb of the burbs. We pulled into the driveway, drove into the garage and walked into the house as we had sat in the car, silent.

"So mom, what's this I hear about you and dad getting a divorce?"

"I . . . I've . . . I've been meaning to talk to you about that . . ."

"When exactly did you think you'd be talking to me about it, on my way to the airport?!"

"Well honey . . . I don't know . . . there's really not much to say . . ."

"Not much to say?! Where did you get that? I come all the way from California and spend a week and on my last hour here you finally get around to talking, if you can call it that, and you tell me there 'isn't much to say'?! What the hell is that?"

"You don't talk to me like that, I'm your mother."

It was charging out of me and I had no way to plug the dike.

"This is exactly what's wrong with this family . . . we never talk."

"Nonsense . . ."

"Nonsense? Why is it then, that nobody seems to know what is going on?"

"That's not true?"

"Not true? That's bull . . . !"

"Don't talk to me that way."

"The hell with you mom . . . I'll take a cab to the airport."

The door slammed behind me and the hot sun hit my face equally as hard.

She tried calling a few weeks after the incident.

"Michael?"

"Hi."

"Can we talk?"

"I don't think so mom."

"Why not honey?"

"I just think it would be better if we didn't talk for awhile. I need a little time to sort some things out."

I didn't speak to my mother again for about six months. I blamed her for this tragic failure. I blamed her for everything. The failure of this marriage, the failure of her first marriage to my biological father, the inability to communicate to her children, the break-up of our family, and on and on and on . . .

I did not take into account that perhaps she was miserable in her present relationship or her first marriage. I had never even bothered to ask her in all these years past what had happened to my biological father who had suddenly disappeared from my sight and memory at the impressionably tender age of two. A man whose image had been thoroughly buried in my mother's tight memory vaults. I went from to losing Dad #2, to not knowing Dad #1, to the future or remote possibility of acquiring a "Dad #3."

At the time I was going through my own personal problems [hell], and had moved to a small one room rent controlled apartment in the beach side community of Santa Monica.

I finally made it to the beach, I thought. I stood there feeling empty however. Empty and alone like a kid without a dad.

* * * *

That winter in Los Angeles was as wet as they come. I felt trapped in my crate of an apartment as I watched the thick rain blur the existence of the outdoors. I'd now alienated myself from my family, especially my mother, and started dating a British woman by the name of "Jo."

As the estrangement from my mother started to wear on me, the Brit and I got closer, and I began to share with her the details of the argument I'd had with my mother.

"It's not about your mother you know."

"What are you talking about?"

"Your anger doesn't directly have anything to do with her. It's your father."

"He's not the one who wanted the divorce."

"No stupid . . . not him. Your real dad . . . your biological or whatever you want to call it bloody father."

"Are you suggesting I am angry with my birth father?"

"Do you know who he is?"

"Well . . . I know his name, and she told me once that I looked like him."

"Sounds to me as if you need to talk to her." She had a point. "You know, I never had the opportunity you've got."

"What opportunity is that?"

"Well . . . for all you know, your father is still alive, out there somewhere, perhaps hoping you'll find him someday. My father died when I was three years old. I've always wondered what it would have been like to have grown up with me dad. I'll never have an opportunity to see him again, but you may possibly have that chance."

Did I? I thought. I'd never even imagined what it might have been like to have grown up with my father. Who was he?

I called my newly divorced mother hoping to get answers to questions that were stored in some young, frightened, locked vault inside my head.

"Hello?"

"Mom . . . it's me."

"Hello Mikey, I'm glad you called."

"Listen . . . mom . . . I'm sorry for what I said. I'm sorry I hurt you. I'm sorry I haven't spoken to you in so long. I have some questions I need answered. I . . . I . . . need to know about my father . . . my biological dad."

"What do you want to know? I'll tell you whatever you need to know."

"Who was he? Where did you meet him? When did you marry? What happened? What was . . ."

"Hang on, hang on . . . let me get to these questions first. I've told you his name was John Sidney Woods," It was true, she had. This, and a passing reference that I looked just like him had been my sole fragments of evidence that he existed.

"I met him at school out East when I transferred from the University of Illinois to Boston University. He was a handsome man . . . beautiful . . . I fell in love and then got pregnant."

"Was I a mistake?"

"Mikey, don't use that term honey. That's not right. Maybe you weren't exactly planned, but you were never a mistake. Anyway, we were very young and scared, Sid and I were just kids . . . .Sid . . . that's what everybody called your father."

It suddenly became clear to me . . . that's why I got the name . . . Michael Sidney. It was a tribute to my father.

"I really had no plan. I didn't know what I was doing. I certainly could not go home. I was 19 years old, 20 by the time you were born. I had a friend who had gone out to Los Angeles, so I scraped together all the money I could from my part-time job and bought a one-way ticket to California."

"Did you keep in touch with Sid?"

"I kept writing him and he asked me to come back to Boston as soon as you were born. I went back and we married and lived in the area known as Roxbury, a very poor neighborhood. We didn't have any money so I never knew if we were going to have enough food from day to day, and my Armenian family had disowned me. I was so scared those first years."

"So what happened? Why did we leave?"

"I don't know . . . I guess things just fell apart, we were so poor, and we were just kids. When my mother heard about our situation, she came out to visit and begged me to come home. I knew I couldn't live like that any more so I packed us up and we went to live with your grandparents in Waukegan."

"What happened to my father?"

"We got a divorce, and later I married John Fosberg. Sid called once more when you were about eight or nine years old. You answered the phone and when he asked for me, you handed me the phone. He just called to see how we were doing. I've never spoken to him again."

As I tried to process all of this, I realized what I had to do.

"Mom, I'm going to try and find him."

"What? Why do you want to do that? You have a father . . . John Fosberg. He raised you. He is your father."

"Yes, he is my father, he did raise me . . . I understand that. Look, I don't know how to explain this. It's . . . it's . . . as if I were a large jigsaw puzzle and there is one piece missing. I don't even know if it is a significant piece or not, but I know I need to find it to complete the picture."

"If there's anyway I can help, let me know."

"Do you remember where he was living the last time he called?"

"Well . . . I think he lived in the Detroit area at the time. I'm not sure, but I think that is what I remember him saying."

We went to say our good-bye's and I could still feel my mother's uneasiness mixed with a trace of relief . . . or was it mine?

[types and says] "A COUPLE OF THINGS MY MOTHER NEVER TOLD ME"

A week went by. I sat in my walk-in closet of an apartment weighing the new information my mother had given me. I knew I wanted to find my father, but I was lost as to exactly how to do it. The fear of searching for him, and uncertainty of where to start, caused the already too close walls of my room to close in. I decided to take a walk to the beach.

As I strolled through downtown, past the Santa Monica Public Library, I stopped for a moment. What are the chances that after 25 years, my father could still live in the Detroit area? I turned and went inside the library.

I made my way to the reference section, preparing to "let my fingers do the walking" through the Metro Detroit white pages. I reached for the faded white publication and removed it cautiously from the shelf. [sits at table, looks through phone book] "Woods . . ." [retrieves paper and pencil to copy names] JOHN S. WOODS at 17610 Fairway Dr., phone # (313) 345-5391 . . . JOHN WOODS at 3547 Tilman Avenue, phone # (313) 895-8467 . . . Then, four more listings of JOHN WOODS . . .

I neatly replaced the directory, swiftly made my way for the exit, and raced back the remaining nine blocks to my apartment. Once inside I paced the three steps across and two steps back my hovel afforded me. I laid the piece of paper with the names and numbers on the desk in front of me and tried to sit down and pick up the phone. I grabbed the receiver but could not pick it up. *What if I find him? What will I say? What if he doesn't want to speak to me?*

How will I react? Is it fair of me to impose myself on a man who'd been absent from my life for so many years? What if he has a family and this creates an embarrassing situation? What if none of these names on this list is my father? What do I do next? Do I really want to do this?

It was midafternoon, Detroit was three hours ahead, I needed to make my move. What would I say should someone answer my phone call? Obviously I'm looking for a John Sidney Woods but how many men could have that same name and what would help me determine if he were my father? I'd ask him if he lived in Boston in 1957. Was that enough? How about if he was married to an Armenian woman named Adrienne Pilibosian? An affirmative answer to that question would certainly seal my fate.

Finally I grabbed the receiver and punched in the top number on the list my heart pounding. I heard the phone ring twice and then a click.

"Hello?"

"I . . . I'm . . . I'm looking for a John Sidney Woods?"

"You're speaking with him."

"Did you live in the Boston area in 1957?"

"Yes I did."

"W . . . were you m . . . married to a . . . w . . . woman by the name of Adrienne Pilibosian?"

"Yes . . . I was."

My dad. First call . . . First time. Thirty-one years later.

"My name is Michael Fosberg, and I'm your son! . . ." I suddenly remembered horror stories about kids who found their parents after many years missing, and the parents wanted nothing to do with them. "Look, it's all right if you don't want to talk to me

... I just wanted to find out how you were ... and let you know that I was all right ..."

"*No . . . my God, son . . . how are you? Where are you?*"

"I'm ... I'm fine ... I'm ... I'm good ... I live in Los Angeles."

"And your mother, how is she?"

"She's pretty good, I guess."

"What do you mean, 'you guess'?"

"She just got a divorce and we're not exactly on the best of terms right now."

"Just remember son, she's the only mother you've got. Don't be too hard on her."

"So, how about you, what has your life been like?"

"Well . . . I've been working for Ford Motor Company the last 20 years as a purchasing agent. Before that I was with Chrysler Corporation. I've been married 25 years to a woman named Sue and we have no children."

Thirty years wrapped up into a couple of brief descriptions.

"You know, son, there's a couple of things you need to know that I'm sure your mother never told you."

"What's that?"

"Well, first of all I want you to know that no matter what you were told, or what you thought happened, I have always loved you and thought about you a lot."

For the first time my father, my dad, my biological procreator, my blood, told me that he loved me.

"There's one other thing that I'm sure your mother never told you."

"What?"

"I'm African American."

My body went numb. I felt light-headed. I was standing next to my bureau and my body just sank. I braced myself with my left hand while I continued to hold the phone with my right.

"Your grandparents are Roy and Lois Woods, descendants of the Woods and Robinson families of Columbia and Jefferson City, Missouri, and have been living for the past 40 years in Virginia Beach, Virginia."

"Wow."

"Are you all right?"

"Yes . . . yes . . . I'm fine . . . great really . . . You're right, she never bothered to mention that."

"Your grandfather was the chairman of the science and engineering departments at Norfolk State University and the Science building is named after him. There are unconfirmed stories in the family that his great grandfather, Al Woods was first cousin to John Brown. Your great great grandfather was a member of the 54th regiment of the colored infantry during the Civil War. Your Grandmother's father, Charles 'Lefty' Robinson, was once an all-star pitcher with the Negro Leagues. Your grandmother has four siblings all still alive and well . . ."

I didn't know what to say. I couldn't formulate words let alone sentences. I went from growing up in a white working-class family to being a black man in the blink of an eye. I strained to try to put an image together. What do my grandparents look like? What does he look like? Do I look like him?

"I am very light-skinned and have been told I could almost pass for white, but like most black families, there are all sorts of shades in our blood. I'll put together a couple of pictures and send them your way and maybe you could do the same?"

"Say, listen Dad . . . you do want to keep in touch, don't you?"

"Absolutely, son. I've been hoping you'd get in touch at some point in your life, I was just never sure when it would be. I half expected you years ago when you were in your 20's. We have lots to talk about and plenty of time to do it."

We hung up the phone. "DAMN!" The puzzle was now whole. All my life I couldn't figure out what was wrong with me when nothing was really wrong with me at all. *I'M BLACK, DAMNIT . . . I'M BLACK! AND I KNEW IT ALL ALONG!*

[Music on fast and loud: track 2, "I'm Black, I'm Proud," recites along with it] "I'm black, I'm proud!" [crosses offstage, brings out African figure and sets it down on desk, steps behind desk. Music fades out as he raises his arms]

Not a day went by since that fateful call to my father, when I didn't think about my new found heritage . . . [in an African dialect] de weight of my "black" history . . . de implications of my race . . . [back to natural voice] the pain of my irreclaimable past. My mind was on overload sorting through the assortment of information and emotions. Then I started in on the "what if's" and "if only's" . . . "If only I'd known, before I filled out applications for college! What if Jo wouldn't accept my new-found blackness?"

"Jo, I found my father . . . "

"You can't be serious?!"

" . . . and it turns out he's black."

"BLOODY HELL!"

"I'm black! I spoke to him not more than a hour ago."

"I can't believe your mother never told you."

"I know. Wass up wit dat?"

"No wonder you're so angry with her." She was right. I was angry. I couldn't believe my mother had kept this "secret" from me my entire life, that she would not so much lie, but avoid the truth and deceive me. "Maybe she didn't know he was black?"

As I reached for the phone to call her not knowing what the hell I would say, it rang.

"Hello."

"Foz, it's me, Tommy."

"Tommy?!"

Tommy was an old buddy of mine.

"Hey Tommy, what's up?"

"Nothing buddy. Just callin' to see how you been doin'."

"How funny you should ask . . . you'll never believe what's hap-pened to me . . ." I gave him the condensed version of the "Finding My Father / Black Man in a White Man's Body" story and he said, "I always knew you were black."

How he knew this is beyond me. But Tommy wasn't the only one! How did they know? What did they see? [**Music on under speech: track 3, "Super Bad/Super Fly"**] Maybe it was the fact that I owned practically every James Brown record ever recorded. Or it could've been the phenomenon that I could recite every word of every single Richard Pryor album complete with characterizations, dialects, and facial expressions. Perhaps it was those outfits I wore in high school of platform shoes, multicolored rayon shirts, wide purple corduroy pants, topped off with kinky hair, and a wide brim hat. It may have been as one friend put it; "Foz, you were cooler than cool. Anybody that cool, we knew had to have been from another race!" Or maybe it was my 'fro that got me cast as a mulatto in my first professional show out of college and then they corned-rowed my hair. Or, quite possibly it was a high school girlfriends' parents who upon meeting me one summer with my wild afro and dark tan, pulled her aside in another room and asked her a bit to loudly, [**music stops abruptly**] "Nancy, exactly what nationality is that boy?"

"That's great Foz! Are you gonna meet him?"

"Well sure, I hope so, but not for a while, I guess."

"So what's troubling you?"

"Well . . . I'm angry, man. I can't believe my mother never told me . . . She lied to me Tommy, betrayed me . . . and I don't know what the heck to say to her."

"No Foz . . . don't you see . . . you have an opportunity to absolve your mother of her shame. She was given this shame by her parents, Armenian immigrants, and has held onto it your entire life. You now have a chance to help her let it go . . . to help her release her guilt and shame."

Tommy's words had made me feel my mother's plight for the first time. A 19-year-old first generation Armenian girl away at college in Boston, 1957, falls in love with a black man by whom she becomes suddenly pregnant and instantly disowned by her family. What it must have been like for her to be forced to leave the man she loves, return home to a mostly hostile family environment, and raise her child as a single mother. This was the answer I'd been searching for.

I picked up the phone to call her. Yet after all this, there was still a voice inside me insisting that she didn't know my father was black. She couldn't have. The little boy in me just couldn't believe his mommy had lied to him.

"Hello, mom?"

"Michael?"

"Yeah."

"Are you all right?"

"Yeah, mom." There was a slight nervousness to her questions as if she knew why I had called. "I found my father."

"You did? That's great. That's great. That's what you wanted. Are you happy? That's what you wanted. You found your father. That's what you wanted. Wasn't it? I gotta go now . . ."

"So . . . mom, did you . . . know . . . he was . . . black?"

"Yes."

"So . . . what was that Cherokee Indian thing you told me?"

"I thought he told me his family had Indian blood in it. He was awfully light skinned you know. There must have been some type of light blood in his family. I didn't know what to tell you. I didn't want you growing up confused or ashamed. I didn't want you to grow up resenting me, or yourself for that matter. I sought advice from a therapist and we decided that it was best not to tell you right away, to wait until you got older. As you got older it became harder to tell you. I was afraid you might reject me, be angry with me, resent me. I didn't want to lose you. I'm sorry Michael . . . I didn't . . ."

"You don't have to apologize. You did what you thought was right. You did the best you knew how and that's OK with me. I found my father and I still love you."

"Do you . . . are you . . . do you mean that? Are you sure?"

"Yes mom."

I heard her take a deep breath, and then a sigh. We said our good-bye's and I set the phone down gently in its cradle.

* * * *

[crosses to stage right chairs and lies down]

February 17th, exactly two weeks after I had spoken with my father, 6 a.m. Pacific Standard Time, I was most likely in some sort of dream state at this hour, jarred awake by the familiar sound of the phone.

[sleepily] "Hello."

"Hey shuga, how ya doin'?" Had I heard it correctly, or was I just dreaming? "You still got dem big feets?" Then the voice hit me again as if somehow deeply familiar. "Shuga, you there?"

"Yes." My dream state was replaced with one of instant recognition.

"Where the hell you bin?! We bin expectin' you ten years ago!"

"Granny?"

"Yes shuga . . . it's me. How the hell are ya?"

"I'm great now. I feel like I'm finally home."

"You shore are. Our door has always bin open fo' you. I always thought that if there was any warmth in Adi and the warmth that was in John Sidney, there had ta be warmth in you. I jus' had the feeling that there was enough warmth and closeness that one day there would be a knock at the door and you gon be standin' an wantin' to know is this the residence of the parents of John Sidney Woods."

"Well, knock knock, I'm home. Tell me, how the hell are you?"

"I got no reason ta complain . . . it wouldn't do me no good no how. Once in a while I get a visit from Arthur . . . other den that I'm not bad fo' an old lady."

"Who's Arthur?"

"Oh you know . . . he come creepin' 'round in my hands . . . arthritis . . ."

My 79-year-old, full of joy, Virginia-southern grandmother, Lois E. Woods.

"Can you send me some photographs of you and grandpa?"

"Well shore shuga. I got plenty of photographs of all of us. Lemme look through what I got n' I'll send some yo' way."

We exchanged addresses and numbers and I told her I would like to see her soon.

"Don't you worry shuga, we gonna get together soon, all a us, you, John Sid, Poppa n' me. There's gonna be plenty a time fo that."

I hung up. It was 6:15 a.m. I had just spoken with my African American grandmother for the first time in my life. I was wide awake, sitting straight up in bed, with a warmth about me I'd never experienced.

☆ ☆ ☆ ☆

[returns to desk, takes chair from behind desk and sets it in front of desk]

It is the early part of summer. I'm on a plane to Norfolk, Virginia with my British girlfriend. Our objective is to meet my father, who was flying there from Detroit, and stay with my grandparents.

Jo, the Brit is videotaping our journey with a borrowed camera from dear friends of mine, a black couple who upon hearing my race changing news proclaimed, "Oh, ha, ha ha, we always knew you was one a the family!"

"Are you nervous?" Jo asks me as she focuses the camera on my head from the seat next to me on the plane. I nod in the affirmative and smile sheepishly.

"All right, just checking."

The plane ride, which takes about five and a half hours, seems to be taking ten and a half. Suddenly, a smooth Southern dialect interrupts the airplane chaos.

"Ladies and gentlemen we are approaching the Norfolk/Virginia Beach area. At this time we ask those of you who are up, to return to your race, fasten your seat belts, put your tray tables up, and return your seats to their white positions."

The plane lands.

"It's now or never darling."

I take a deep breath, grab our carry-ons, and head out through the plane.

Once inside the terminal, I scan the crowd and immediately spot my grandmother. She is a large beautiful light-skinned black woman with thinning gray hair and round glasses. She waves at me across the terminal as I race toward her and embrace all of her with my long arms.

We are locked in a clinch, oblivious to the airport clamor surrounding us.

When we release our grip, we notice Jo has circled with the camera and is now facing us.

My grandmother and I walk arm in arm toward the baggage claim, smiling and laughing through our tears, camera crew in tow.

At the baggage claim turnstile I grab a bag that appears to be ours.

"Here comes Poppa."

I turn and find myself practically eye to eye with a tall husky handsome older black man. It is my grandfather. Roy A. Woods. I drop the bag, we shake hands, and I wrap my free arm around his shoulder. He is visibly annoyed by the Brit with the circling camera, but smiles warmly and says little.

"Hey Lee."

"What?"

"I say hey Lee."

"What are you talking about?"

"You n' your father."

"What do you mean?"

"Yo father UG . . . n' you LEE . . . n' between the two a ya's, you the UG . . . LEE twins!"

✳ ✳ ✳ ✳

The following morning, we wake up late and arise to find my grandmother busy in the kitchen.

"Poppa's gone to the airport to get your daddy. Y'all grab yo'self sumthin to eat n' sit down fo he get back."

"Well, what are you doin' there Granny?"

"Jus getting things together fo supper tonight. Y'all work around me."

When we finish our breakfast we have a seat in the family room area. Suddenly Granny looks toward the entry and a smile moves across her face.

"They're home."

Jo quickly mans the video camera as each of us stand there in a kind of awkward anticipatory moment. I hear the door open and then shut. Finally, thirty years later my father enters the room.

He looks over at Jo running the video.

"Hey there sweetheart, you got the camera going."

He turns and faces me and we stand eye to eye, both somewhat unsure, both in amazement. I look exactly like him . . . same smile, same hair, same way he moves his hands, same tilt of his head, the same resonance in his voice.

"Jesus Christ . . . you're a good lookin' kid!"

We stand examining each other. I can feel the jubilation around the room although my attention is completely on the man, the mirror in front of me.

"Come here, (arms out) and give your old man a hug."

The reunion is complete.

Later that evening my grandmother has prepared a sumptuous, soulful, southern meal of fried catfish, collard greens, macaroni and cheese, sweet potatoes, and cornbread. It is the best food I have ever tasted.

※ ※ ※ ※

[sits at desk, types and says] "The Inkwell."

I finally made it West Coast to East after having tape-recorded interviews with family members both black and white. I'm on Martha's Vineyard. It is a spectacular day, bright blue sky with scattered creamy clouds. I've come to visit a cousin, Cheryl, a second cousin who played a significant role during my early childhood.

We've arranged to meet for a late lunch. When I arrive I notice her immediately, seated on a bench outside the appointed restaurant.

She says she wants to drive to the beach, and when we arrive at the particular one she'd been in search of, we circled the parking lots, desperate for an empty space.

"It's awfully crowded here. Are you sure you don't want to try another beach?"

"Honey . . . there is no other beach on this island!"

I knew there were plenty of beaches on the island so this must have some special significance that I was yet unaware of.

"You don't come to the Vineyard and not visit the Inkwell, baby!"

The Inkwell, the infamous "Inkwell," the number one vacation spot for African American families for decades, the beach immortalized in the 1994 Hollywood movie with the same name.

As we step from the car after finally scoring a choice parking spot up front, the beach unfolds in front of me. It is packed with every shade of black person you can imagine. It looked like "Soul Train" meets "MTV" . . . people dancing, laughing, joking, struttin' their stuff.

Cheryl began calling out to folks and before I knew what was happening, dozens of people were stepping up to say hello.

"Donitra, this my cousin Michael from Chicago . . ."

"Chicago huh? I gots family from up near round there, where you stay?"

"Well . . . I don't actually live there at the moment. I live out in LA."

"California! I know you gots to be lovin' dat!"

A distinguished looking gentleman approaches us.

"Hey Skip, how ya doin'?"

"I'm good thanks Cheryl . . . how's by you?"

"Real good. Skip I want you to meet my cousin Michael. Michael Fosberg, Henry Louis Gates Jr."

I choked momentarily as I recognized the name to be that of one of the country's foremost black intellectuals and a writer from Harvard University. I grabbed his hand awkwardly. "Mr. Gates . . . ."

"Skip . . . Nice to meet you Michael."

"It's a pleasure to meet you sir."

There is waving and laughter, jokes and stories, a few handshakes, slaps, and hugs.

"Hey Shirelle, this is my cousin Michael . . ."

"Hey Michael, how ya doin' baby?"

Does she know everyone? "I'm doin' great thanks."

"Baby, we throwin' a party tamara night. What chu doin'?"

"Ah jees, I'm going back home tomorrow morning . . ."

"Oh no baby, you can change dat . . . you gots ta party with us!"

"Well . . . I'll see what I can do . . ."

"We gon bring the house down baby. You gon wanna piece a dat!"

"Yeah . . .sure . . ."

In that instant I suddenly have a vision of what my life may have been like; summers on the Vineyard, the Inkwell, the parties, hanging with the sista's. As I revel silently in the joy of those images, in the same BREATH . . .

I realize the other side of that picture . . . confusion, racism, hardship, ridicule, not knowing where I stood; white or black. Where and how would I have fit in? What "race" am I? Am I white? Am I Black?

Did you know when you first saw me? Did you guess? When I made the discovery did you start to look at me differently? Did my nose flatten out? Did my lips get bigger? How did your perception change? And how many different perceptions might there be amongst you, between whites and blacks.

Look, I'm just a guy who went out one day to search for his father. For thirty years my sole source of history, of self, was the rich Armenian heritage my mother's parents surrounded me with. I asked my mother about that time while in Boston when her mother came out secretly visiting us while my father was at work. Upon seeing our impoverished situation, she begged us to return home.

"What if I'd had darker skin Mom?"

"We would probably have never returned home to live with my parents. Your life, our lives, would have been entirely different."

In the end, I was not raised black. I didn't live through the black experience, I was not a target of racism, was not singled out because of the color of my skin, and was not turned away from or called names. Does that make me any less a black man? Do you have to have that experience to be black? All my life I've worn a disguise, a mask of identity. *Incognito* is defined in the dictionary as an adverb meaning *"with the real identity concealed . . . with one's identity hidden or unknown."*

So what am I now? Who am I? Which box do I check off on applications, or the Census? Caucasian? African American? Mixed? Biracial? Multiracial? Mulatto? Octoroon? High Yella? How 'bout triple "A" . . . African American Armenian! Is there a box for that? Or, more importantly, do I need a box to fit in? Frankly, there isn't a box big enough for me to fit in. I've got too much history, too much family, and far too much culture to stick my roots in some box.

I slide between worlds, between cultures experiencing everything from both sides. I live in-between. I walk both sides. A box doesn't tell you who I am. I'm more than a label. I'm more than a race. I'm a kid with two dads . . . with three heritages. I am . . . Michael Sidney . . . Pilibosian Woods Fosberg.

[unrolls a large photo poster and hangs it from desk]

The picture is now complete.

[Music on fast and loud: track 4, "I Got You, I Feel Good"]

CREDITS

Daniel Lanois, "The Unbreakable Chain," *For the Beauty of Wynona* (1993).

James Brown and Alfred Ellis, "Say It Loud—I'm Black and I'm Proud," *A Soulful Christmas* (1968).

James Brown, "Super Bad" (single, 1970).

James Brown, "I Got You (I Feel Good)," *Out of Sight* (1965).

ACKNOWLEDGMENTS

First and foremost I would like to thank all the schools (middle and high schools, colleges and universities) who have hosted me and my show over the years. Without having had the opportunity to present my show and engage students, faculty, and administrators in dialogue, I would not have been able to learn all these things about how we do and don't talk about race and identity.

I would like to thank all the corporations whose personnel were able to wrap their heads around what I was trying to do and who invited me in to perform and conduct dialogue. A one-man play is a tough sell to the CEO, but the show has never failed to prove its value in provoking meaningful dialogue.

Thanks to all the government agencies who also took that extra leap of trusting that the play would pay dividends for their staff. I am personally rewarded each time I visit, engage with folks in robust conversations, and walk away amazed by people's response.

Thanks to those colleagues—both in the diversity and inclusion field and outside—who, over many years of touring and presenting, have been unbelievably encouraging, supportive, and essential to the success of *Incognito*.

And thanks to those who have offered help and advice along the way: Linda Stokes, Jake Cohen, Mark Spector, David O'Donnell, Ned Doheny, Adrian Danzig, Larry Grimm, Ancella Livers, Lindy Williams, Katherine Smith, Carlton Yearwood, Melissa Donaldson, Darlene Slaughter, Philomena Morrissey-Satre, Michael C. Ford, Stuart Hennessey, Lorraine Cole, James

Harris, Andrea Kelton-Harris, Traci Fuller, Elaina Andrade, Kevin Bradley, Cheryl Duncan, Wanda Feldman, Jane Nicholl Sahlins, Bobby Gordon, Allan Partin, Reena Hajat Carroll, Josh Harris, Suzanne Penn, and Clover Morell. Enormous thanks to Siobhan Drummond of Drummond Books for her editing and proofreading expertise.

A big thanks to my invaluable assistant and coconspirator Barbara Harris.

And finally, I could not do what I do if it were not for the love, support, and enormous encouragement of my wife, Jenny Avery.

BIBLIOGRAPHY

Alexander, Michelle. *The New Jim Crow: Mass Incarceration in the Age of Colorblindness*. New York: The New Press, 2010.

Allport, Gordon W. *The Nature of Prejudice*. New York: Perseus Books, 1979.

Anderson, Carol. *White Rage: The Unspoken Truth of Our Racial Divide*. New York: Bloomsbury, 2017.

Asim, Jabari. *The N Word: Who Can Say It, Who Shouldn't, and Why*. New York: Houghton Mifflin, 2007.

Balakian, Peter. *Black Dog of Fate: A Memoir*. New York: Basic Books, 1997.

Balakian, Peter. *The Burning Tigris: The Armenian Genocide and America's Response*. New York: HarperCollins, 2003.

Baldwin, James. *The Fire Next Time*. New York: Dial Press, 1962.

Beatty, Paul. *The White Boy Shuffle: A Novel*. New York: Henry Holt, 1996.

Beatty, Paul. *The Sellout: A Novel*. New York: Farrar, Straus and Giroux, 2015.

Biss, Eula. *Notes from No Man's Land: American Essays*. Minneapolis: Graywolf Press, 2009.

Broyard, Bliss. *One Drop: My Father's Hidden Life—A Story of Race and Family Secrets*. New York: Little, Brown, 2007.

Chang, Jeff. *We Gon' Be Alright: Notes on Race and Resegregation*. New York: Macmillan, 2016.

Coates, Ta-Nehisi. *Between the World and Me*. New York: Random House, 2015.

Coates, Ta-Nehisi. *We Were Eight Years in Power: An American Tragedy.* New York: Random House, 2017.

Crouch, Stanley. *The All-American Skin Game, or The Decoy of Race: The Long and the Short of It, 1990–1994.* New York: Pantheon, 1995.

Du Bois, W. E. B. *The Souls of Black Folk.* New York: Dover, 1994.

Dyson, Michael Eric. *Tears We Cannot Stop: A Sermon to White America.* New York: St. Martin's Press, 2017.

Early, Gerald, ed. *Lure and Loathing: Essays on Race, Identity, and the Ambivalence of Assimilation.* New York: Penguin, 1994.

Edugyan, Esi. *Washington Black.* New York: Penguin Random House, 2018.

Haizlip, Shirlee Taylor. *The Sweeter the Juice: A Family Memoir in Black and White.* New York: Simon and Schuster, 1995.

Haley, Alex. *The Autobiography of Malcolm X.* New York: Random House, 1964.

Hobbs, Jeff. *The Short and Tragic Life of Robert Peace: A Brilliant Young Man Who Left Newark for the Ivy League.* New York: Simon and Schuster, 2014.

Holliday, Laurel. *Children of the Dream: Our Own Stories of Growing Up Black in America.* New York: Simon and Schuster, 1999.

Johnson, James Weldon. *The Autobiography of an Ex-Colored Man.* Boston: Sherman, French, 1912.

Johnson, Mat. *Loving Day: A Novel.* New York: Spiegel and Grau, 2016.

Jordan, Winthrop D. *White over Black: American Attitudes Towards the Negro 1550–1812.* New York: Penguin, 1973.

Kendi, Ibram X. *Stamped from the Beginning: The Definitive History of Racist Ideas in America.* New York: Nation Books, 2016.

Lewis, Sinclair. *Kingsblood Royal.* New York: Random House, 2001. Originally published 1947.

Maalouf, Amin. *In the Name of Identity: Violence and the Need to Belong.* Translated by Barbara Bray. New York: Penguin, 2003.

Mandela, Nelson. *Long Walk to Freedom.* New York: Back Bay Books, 1995.

McBride, James. *The Color of Water: A Black Man's Tribute to His White Mother.* New York: Penguin, 1996.

McBride, James. *The Good Lord Bird: A Novel.* New York: Penguin, 2013.

Murray, Albert. *The Omni-Americans: Some Alternatives to the Folklore of White Supremacy.* New York: Outerbridge and Dienstfrey, 1970.

Rankine, Claudia. *Citizen: An American Lyric.* Minneapolis: Graywolf Press, 2014.

Rothstein, Richard. *The Color of Law: A Forgotten History of How Our Government Segregated America.* New York: W. W. Norton, 2017.

Russell, Dick. *Black Genius: Inspirational Portraits of African-American Leaders.* New York: Skyhorse, 2009.

Shipler, David K. *A Country of Strangers: Blacks and Whites in America.* New York: Alfred A. Knopf, 1997.

Skyhorse, Brando, and Lisa Page, eds. *We Wear the Mask: Fifteen True Stories of Passing in America.* Boston: Beacon, 2017.

Smith, Zadie. *White Teeth: A Novel.* New York: Random House, 2000.

Smith, Zadie. *On Beauty: A Novel.* New York: Penguin, 2005.

Solomon, Andrew. *Far from the Tree: Parents, Children, and the Search for Identity.* New York: Simon and Schuster, 2012.

Steele, Claude M. *Whistling Vivaldi: How Stereotypes Affect Us and What We Can Do.* New York: W. W. Norton, 2010.

Suskind, Ron. *A Hope in the Unseen: An American Odyssey from the Inner City to the Ivy League.* New York: Random House, 1999.

Taibbi, Matt. *I Can't Breathe: A Killing on Bay Street.* New York: Spiegel and Grau, 2017.

Tatum, Beverly Daniel. *Why Are All the Black Kids Sitting Together in the Cafeteria? And Other Conversations about Race.* New York: Basic Books, 1997.

Toomer, Jean. *Cane.* New York: W. W. Norton, 2011. Originally published 1923.

Twain, Mark. *Pudd'nhead Wilson.* New York: Penguin, 1986. Originally published 1894.

Walker, Rebecca. *Black, White, and Jewish: Autobiography of a Shifting Self.* New York: Riverhead Books, 2001.

Washington, Booker T. *The Negro Problem.* New York: J. Pott and Co., 1903.

West, Cornel. *Hope on a Tightrope: Words and Wisdom.* Carlsbad, CA: Smiley Books, 2008.

Whitehead, Colson. *The Underground Railroad: A Novel.* New York: Penguin Random House, 2016.

Whitehead, Colson. *The Nickel Boys: A Novel.* New York: Penguin Random House, 2019.

Whitman, James Q. *Hitler's American Model: The United States and the Making of Nazi Race Law.* Princeton, NJ: Princeton University Press, 2017.

Wideman, John Edgar. *Brothers and Keepers: A Memoir.* New York: Houghton Mifflin Harcourt, 1984.

Wideman, John Edgar. *Fatheralong: A Meditation on Fathers and Sons.* New York: Random House, 1994.

Wilkerson, Isabel. *The Warmth of Other Suns: The Epic Story of America's Great Migration.* New York: Random House, 2010.

Winters, Ben H. *Underground Airlines: A Novel.* New York: Hachette, 2016.

Wise, Tim. *White Like Me: Reflections on Race from a Privileged Son.* Berkeley, CA: Counterpoint, 2008.

ABOUT THE AUTHOR

Chicago native Michael Fosberg has spoken at nearly a thousand high schools, colleges, government agencies, corporations, and not-for-profits since 2001, utilizing his award-winning autobiographical story as an entry point for meaningful dialogues on race and identity. He has collaborated with a number of professional diversity practitioners on programs to foster deeper dialogue in corporate settings and at educational institutions. His work with groups such as the Boeing Company, United Way Worldwide, PNC Financial Services, Proctor and Gamble, Harvard College, the US Department of the Treasury, and the Immigration and Customs Enforcement Agency is reshaping the way organizations talk about race, identity, and diversity. Michael has been a frequent guest in the media, speaking on issues of race, identity, stereotypes, diversity, inclusion, and unconscious bias, to name just a few topics. His first book, *Incognito: An American Odyssey of Race and Self-Discovery*, was published in 2011 and chronicles his personal journey to find his biological father.

Information about Michael Fosberg, his memoir, the play, and his unique diversity training offerings can be found at:

www.incognitotheplay.com

Although the play is by far his most requested offering, he also has been asked to give speeches and has sat on panels discussing issues of race and identity. For more information and requests for presentations, you can write to him at:

Michael@incognitotheplay.com